Bill Owens'
Buffalo Bill's Brewery
and Other Adventures

by Pat Walls

White Mule Press a division of the
American Distilling Institute
PO Box 577
Hayward, CA 94541
whitemulepress.com

ISBN 978-0-9968277-7-5

To Sarah and Althea

Contents

INTRODUCTION

Craft beer is not just another consumer good; it is a reflection of the American Dream. Beer enthusiasts choose to imbibe craft beer because it is an affordable and accessible luxury that is more flavorful than mass-market, light, fizzy lagers.[1] The majority of United States brewery owners enter the brewing industry as beer enthusiasts and homebrewers, seeking the opportunity to create a successful business by recreating flavors and beer styles that initially ignited their passion while also creating new flavors and new styles. Craft beer culture is more than the relationship between producers and consumers; it encompasses everything from apparel and glassware, festivals and competitions, brewery events and food pairing dinners, to hundreds of print publications and review websites. Craft beer has millions of devoted followers searching for fresh, authentic beer.

The Brewers Association, the not-for-profit trade group that promotes American craft brewing, defines craft brewers as "small, independent, and traditional."[2] Brewery size is measured by number of barrels brewed per year, with 31 gallons per barrel. Craft brewers are small as they brew fewer than 6 million barrels per year whereas the largest brewery in the world, Anheuser-Busch InBev, brewed over 389 million barrels in 2015.[3] Craft brewers are independent with less than 25 percent ownership by large, non-craft brewers unlike, for example, Blue Moon, which is wholly owned by MillerCoors. Craft brewers brew the majority of their beer where the flavor comes from using traditional brewing techniques and ingredients. In 2015, 4,269 breweries operated in the United States (1,650 brewpubs, 2,397 microbreweries, 178 regional craft breweries, and 44 non-craft breweries), with craft breweries averaging less than 5,800 barrels per year.[4] The Brewers Association defines different categories of craft breweries based on their production and sales location. A Brewpub is "[a] restaurant-brewery that sells 25 percent or more of its beer on site."[5] Brewpubs serve fresh-made beer to their immediate, local communities. Microbreweries produce up to 15,000 barrels per year with up to 75 percent sold off-site at bars, restaurants, or stores, most often limited to their local area, home state, or nearby states. Regional craft breweries produce between 15,000 and 6,000,000 barrels per year and are (most often) available in multiple states and possibly multiple countries.[6] Regional craft breweries often begin as microbreweries but increase their production and geographic reach over time.

The number of breweries in the United States has deviated over time. In 1873 the number peaked at 4,131, serving 8.9 million barrels of beer to approximately 42 million people, averaging 1 barrel per 4.7 people and 10,167 people per brewery.[7] Through aggressive brewery consolidation, changes in consumer preferences, and societal changes (notably the temperance movement leading to Prohibition), the number of breweries steadily declined.[8] In 1982, 93 breweries operated across the United States, mostly regional breweries making a similar commodity good serving over 231 million people, or 2.5 million people per brewery. Craft beer has experienced explosive growth as consumers experience new and unique products. The number of US breweries surpassed the 1873 historic high of 4,131 in November 2015, with growth currently exceeding two breweries opening every day.[9] Craft beer grossed $22,300,000,000 in 2015, or 21% of the total US beer market, a 16% growth over 2014. The industry produced 24,523,015 barrels or 13% of beer production in 2015, a 15% increase over 2014.[10] Breweries and brewpubs employ over 115,000 people while auxiliary businesses (such as alcohol wholesalers, retailers, restaurants, farmers, and equipment and merchandise manufacturers) employ over 300,000 people.[11] Craft beer is a major economic force in the United States.

Most academic work on craft beer focuses on the industry's economic impact. Since craft beer's beginning in the mid-1960s, many of the pioneering brewers are still alive, continually giving interviews to interested beer writers, journalists, and historians. Maureen Ogle's *Ambitious Brew: The Story of American Beer* is the first comprehensive academic history of the U.S. beer industry. Tom Acitelli's *The Audacity of Hops: The History of America's Craft Beer Revolution* is the first book to focus solely on craft beer's history. All other history books on beer focus on specific companies such as Dan Baum's *Citizen Coors: A Grand Family Saga of Business, Politics, and Beer* or William Knoedelseder's *Bitter Brew: The Rise and Fall of Anheuser-Busch and America's Kings of Beer*. Many are written as first-person accounts such as Philip Van Munching's *Beer Blast: The Inside Story of the Brewing Industry's Bizarre Battles for Your Money* and autobiographies from the founders of Sierra Nevada, Brooklyn Brewing, Dogfish Head, Lagunitas, and Samuel Adams among others.[12]

Many beer journalists touch on the history of craft beer in articles focused on industry news for magazines, newspapers, and online forums including *Ale Street News, All About Beer, American Brewer, BeerAdvocate, Craft Beer & Brewing, Draft Magazine, Northwest Brewing News*, and *The Celebrator Beer News*. The final type of beer writing that explores beer's history focuses on brewing different beer styles in books and journals including *Brew Your Own, Zymurgy Magazine*, and *The New Brewer*. The latter two magazines are published by the Brewers Association which has an ever-increasing roster of books on beer styles, recipes, and brewery operations.[13] Most beer writers start as beer fans who want to share their passion and find or create avenues to do so, but many do not follow academic (or sometimes journalistic) rigor. The better beer writers, including Michael Jackson, Fred Eckhardt, Charlie Papazian, Garrett Oliver, Randy Mosher, and Stan Hieronymus, rise above others to be seen as experts in the field of beer and beer writing.

Craft beer's ascendency is due to the innovative efforts of pioneering brewers and writers. Bill Owens was one such pioneer who foresaw the growth of small, local breweries because he wanted access to fresh beer and be the first brewpub owner. As an author, brewer, and publisher, he was one of the nascent industry's biggest advocates and most vocal proponents. Bill Owens is a pioneer in the United States craft brewing industry through his efforts as an advocate, writer, publisher, brewer, and entrepreneur who created a lasting legacy by influencing generations of brewers and beer fans.

Chapter one explores the beer scene prior to Bill Owens' entrance in 1982. Chapter two introduces Owens and traces his pioneering efforts in brewing and writing about beer. Chapter three highlights Owens' expansion and contraction in the industry, while chapter four illustrates Owens' influential publication empire.

As a pioneer, Bill Owens wrote one of the first books focusing on homebrew equipment, advocated for the legalization of brewpubs, owned and operated three of the first brewpubs in the country, recreated and popularized numerous beer styles, and published two industry magazines. While he is recognized as a leader of the early craft beer movement by his peers and an older generation of beer drinkers, Owens is little known by current-day beer fans because he sold his breweries and magazines and exited the craft beer industry in 2001 while his contemporaries continued to grow and expand. Owens' legacy is felt, however, in every aspect of the modern craft beer movement.

CHAPTER ONE
The Beer Scene before 1982

The four traditional ingredients in beer are malted barley, hops, water, and yeast. Barley is allowed to germinate, naturally converting starches into sugars, then roasted to stop the conversion. The length of roasting affects the flavor and color of both the malted barley and the finished beer. For example, lighter malt can impart biscuit and cracker flavors while darker malt can add notes of caramel and chocolate. Different types of malts are mixed together to create the grain bill or soul of beer.[14] Hops are the other flavoring agent in beer, used to add bitterness, round out the sweetness of the malt, and act as a preservative for the finished product. Hops come in many varieties, each contributing slightly different flavors and aromas to the finished beer including pine, grass, citrus, tropical fruit, and even cheese.[15] Yeast ferments the converted sugars from the malt into alcohol, carbon dioxide, and a variety of flavorful by-products.[16] Ale yeast and lager yeast are the two main varieties of brewer's yeast. Ale yeast ferments at warmer temperatures, contributing flavor and aroma compounds to the finished beer. Lager yeast ferments at colder temperatures and imparts little flavor to the finished beer, instead letting the malt and hops dominate. Water is the main ingredient of beer but by no means the simplest. Water chemistry affects how the malt, hops, and yeast interact with one another as much as the brewing process itself. A variety of chemicals can be used to adjust water chemistry to meet the needs of specific beer styles.[17]

Initially, beer differed region by region based on the locally available malt, hops, yeast, and water. Over time new styles emerged with new industrial processes utilizing new agricultural and scientific discoveries. Throughout the twentieth century there were hundreds of beer styles being produced in Europe, Asia, and Africa; however, in the United States most breweries created one style of light, slightly-hopped lager.[18] The United States beer revival was a reintroduction of existing styles in pursuit of better beer.

The United States beer revival is often attributed to two brewers: Fritz Maytag purchasing the faltering, iconic Anchor Brewing Company in 1965 in San Francisco, California and Jack McAuliffe opening the first microbrewery, New Albion Brewing, in 1976 in Sonoma, California. These brewers set a pattern for other craft breweries to be small, independent, and traditional, and they created a legacy of brewers helping one another. Other pioneers of the brewing revival are the many homebrewers, writers, and lawmakers who helped create the culture of craft beer.

Anchor Brewery was the only brewery still making steam beer, a unique California style that uses lager yeast at warm temperatures, which creates a uniquely flavored, amber colored, and highly-carbonated beer. Most other breweries in the U.S. made lightly flavored, lightly colored, and lightly carbonated lagers such as Budweiser. Anchor had been open since 1896, but was barely operational in the mid-1960s and was about to be closed when Maytag bought the historic San Francisco brewery.[19] Though Maytag had no previous brewing experience, he revitalized the brewery and slowly re-introduced beer styles that were not being brewed by other *American breweries* at that time.[20]

Maytag deliberately focused on brewing in small batches, staying independent, and using traditional ingredients and techniques because, as he said, "[w]e had a feeling that we had a better mousetrap and the world would lead a path to its door."[21] Part of that mousetrap was the decision to bottle Anchor Steam in 1971, allowing it to be tasted by curious beer drinkers further afield than the bars and restaurants in the Bay Area.[22] Unlike the sterile, impersonal factories of large breweries, Maytag welcomed visitors to tour the brewery and to "talk shop." He created a roadmap for generations of brewers by offering products that differed from the mass-produced lagers and by mentoring and offering advice to future brewers.

Jack McAuliffe was decidedly not influenced by Anchor Brewery.[23] McAuliffe's New Albion Brewery opened in 1976 in Sonoma, California, an hour drive from Anchor Brewing, and used repurposed dairy and soda industry equipment. Truly independent, McAuliffe recreated the pale ale, porter, and stout styles he discovered and enjoyed while serving in the Navy in Scotland and England, styles he first started homebrewing while overseas.[24] McAuliffe hand-bottled his beer and self-distributed it, driving between bars and restaurants in the Bay Area to deliver beer from his trunk. Since his products and operations were so unique, and because he explicitly marketed brewery tours so visitors could see how the beer was made, interested beer drinkers flocked to his old fruit warehouse brewery.[25] After visiting Anchor Brewing and New Albion Brewery in 1978, Ken Grossman and Paul Camusi, the founders of Sierra Nevada Brewing Company, noted that McAuliffe's brewery worked with "[a] little elbow grease, some start-up capital, [and] a willingness [...] work tortuous [*sic*] hours."[26] Unfortunately, McAuliffe's brewery closed in 1983 due to too much elbow grease, too little capital, and too many torturous hours.[27] Fred Eckhardt wrote, however, his legacy was already in place, inspiring a generation of do-it-yourself brewers.[28] He established the pattern of being inspired by European beer styles and trying to emulate them, first at home and then on a commercial level.

Ken Grossman felt called to beer by his first taste of Anchor Steam which led him to homebrew beer and study chemistry for years before opening a homebrew supply shop and then, with Paul Camusi, Sierra Nevada Brewing Company in 1979. Grossman and Camusi were the first generation of brewers influenced by Maytag and McAuliffe, and would subsequently influence many other brewers, particularly with their pale ale, which created the "West Coast" style for its assertive hoppiness that defined American craft beer.[29] The pattern of homebrewers being influenced by the early breweries, scaling up recipes, and building equipment to open up their own breweries was now in place.

McAuliffe and Grossman, along with generations of brewers since, sought help from Dr. Michael Lewis at the University of California, Davis, where he started the only on-campus brewing education program in the United States in 1964.[30] Dr. Lewis' brewing science classes aimed at maximizing the efficiency of brewing a commodity good for breweries such as Pabst and Anheuser-Busch. McAuliffe and Grossman needed help scaling five gallon homebrew recipes to 230 gallon large-scale recipes since malt, hop, and yeast utilization do not scale linearly.[31] In addition to creating the brewing science undergraduate and graduate program at UC Davis, Dr. Lewis created a Professional Brewing program through UC Davis Extension aimed at the growing craft industry.[32] Dr. Lewis established the American Brewers Guild to educate working or would-be brewers. He also ran the Pub Brewing Company and Lewis Consulting to help small brewers set up their business.[33] As Dick Cantwell, a longtime brewer, beer writer, and current Brewers Association Quality Ambassador wrote in 1995,

> In an industry of informality, where nicknames and forms of address would seem to make us all drinking buddies, it has always seemed somewhat anomalous that Michael Lewis of the University of California at Davis would nearly universally be referred to as "Dr. Lewis." It is as though he alone has occupied the throne of respect rendering the use of a first name inappropriate—no Joe or Bill or Ilse for him—Dr. Lewis is

the only name to be used. It isn't that he doesn't deserve it—or that they don't—it's always simple struck me as funny.[34]

Finding materials, equipment, and information was difficult. Homebrewers found supplies and literature at homebrew shops and winemaking stores. Packets of generic yeast and hopped malted barley extract were sold at small retail locations around the country with limited reach and through mail-order companies, whose catalogues were only available at the shops. The storeowners offered mimeographed recipes for various European beer styles. These recipes were collected by early homebrewers and beer writers such as Fred Eckhardt, who published *A Treatise on Lager Beers* in 1969 and self-published *Amateur Brewer*, a semi-regular journal about homebrewing, which was distributed at homebrew shops.[35] Other influential homebrewers, homebrew shops owners, and writers were Lee Coe, Byron Burch, and Charlie Papazian. Coe taught homebrewing classes and published *The Beginner's Home Brew Book* in 1972 when homebrewing was still illegal. He was an original member of the first two homebrew clubs in the country, the Maltose Falcons in Los Angeles and the Draught Board in San Leandro, California.[36] Burch worked at a homebrew and winemaking supply store in Berkeley, California, and later owned two stores further north in Santa Rosa. He wrote *Quality Brewing: A Guidebook for the Home Production of Fine Beers* in 1974.[37] Papazian began teaching homebrewing in Boulder, Colorado, and first published *The Joy of Homebrewing* in 1976. He later started the homebrewing magazine *Zymurgy* and the trade magazine *New Brewer*. Papazian created the American Homebrewers Association and the in 1978, the Great American Beer Festival (the largest beer event in the US) in 1982, and the Brewers Association (the US craft beer trade organization).[38] These four writers and their publications, along with many others, continue to influence amateur brewers, many of whom made the transition to professional brewing.

Homebrewing, however, was illegal in the United States until 1978. California State Assemblyman Tom Bates of Berkeley wrote the Bates Bill that legalized homebrewing in California and the bill was signed by Governor Jerry Brown. Prior to the bill's passage, individuals were required to pay $828 for a license if they wanted to brew beer for private consumption. While no one actually ever paid the license fee nor did anyone get fined or arrested, the law was necessary to legitimize homebrewing. Berkeley folk singer Helen LaRoza wrote "The Home Brew Victory Song" to celebrate its passage, with lyrics like "We can now make beer in California! They've legalized our brewing it at home!"[39]

Senator Alan Cranston of Palo Alto, California, used Bates' bill as a model to propose HR 1337 and legalized homebrewing at the national level.[40] President Jimmy Carter signed the Cranston Bill on October 14, 1978. The bill allowed adults to legally brew up to 100 gallons of beer per year for personal and family use. Lee Coe worked with both Bates and Cranston to legalize homebrewing.[41]

By 1982 a handful of small, independent breweries existed, most on the West Coast. While the businesses were new, the products were revolutionary. These breweries differentiated their beer from the mass-market products. As Garrett Oliver, a noted beer writer and brewer, said, "[i]nstead of pale yellow bland lagers, they brewed bold chocolaty stouts, snappy bitter India pale ales, and caramel-accented amber ales."[42] The breweries hand-bottled or kegged and self-distributed their beers to nearby bars and restaurants. It was illegal to sell beer directly to consumers due to the three-tier system put in place after Prohibition. The three tiers are producer (brewer), distributor, and retailer (bars, restaurants, and stores). The system was meant to prevent the widespread abuse of tied houses in the late-nineteenth and early-twentieth centuries. Initially, a tied house was a bar or pub in the UK that served only one brewery's products by mutual agreement, metaphorically tying the two separate businesses together.[43] In the US, the mutual agreements morphed until breweries monopolized saloon beer taps through a pay-to-play system (buying exclusive rights to taps), used unsavory sales promotions, or owned saloons outright. Tied house abuses contributed to the passage of Prohibition in 1917.[44] Before Prohibition there were 1,392 breweries, after the passage of the Twenty-first Amendment repealing Prohibition on March 22, 1933, only 164 remained. Most breweries survived Prohibition by purportedly bottling soda or making malt extract for baking.[45] These remaining breweries continued to consolidate or close before 1982, in part because they could not serve customers directly. However, beginning with New Albion, Jack McAuliffe would charge visitors for a sample of his beer.[46]

The emerging breweries did not have the money or manpower to distribute far afield as they brewed small batches in used dairy equipment or grundy tanks. Grundy tanks were 8.5-barrel tanks (263.5 gallons) that were distributed by large UK breweries to UK pubs to be large serving tanks that stored beer under pressure in the cellar. As UK pubs began using keg and bottles, they sold the used grundy tanks to US craft brewers who repurposed the tanks as kettles, fermenters, conditioning tanks, and serving tanks.[47] By brewing in limited quantities, craft brewers could not compete with large breweries in economies of scale, so they relied on their superior product at a higher price. As Charlie Papazian said, "What we were missing until the homebrewing revival and the emergence of small and independent craft brewers and their craft beers was, sadly, choice. The economics of mass marketing had indeed influenced what was offered."[48] While craft brewers offered more choice of diverse beer styles, they were still limited in where they could sell their products. In 1982, that was about to change.

CHAPTER TWO
Brewing Change, 1982-1985

Like many craft brewers before and after him, brewing was not Bill Owens' first or second career choice. Owens was born in San José, California in 1938, and he grew up in a farming community outside of Sacramento. He struggled through school due to dyslexia and dreamt of visiting the far-off places he read about in his favorite book, Richard Halliburton's *The Complete Book of Marvels*.[49] After flunking out of Chico State College, Owens hitchhiked to see the world's marvels firsthand before he served as a Peace Corps Volunteer in Jamaica between 1964 and 1966. It was in Jamaica that he discovered his love of photography, capturing how individuals engage with their surroundings, and set him on his first career path. Upon returning to California, Owens finished his teaching credential at Chico State College then took courses in visual anthropology and documentary photography from Jack Collier at San Francisco State University, the author of the definitive textbook *Visual Anthropology: Photography as a Research Method*.[50]

In 1968 and while living in Livermore, Owens got his first photography job as a staff photographer at *The Livermore Independent* in the growing suburban communities of the eastern Bay Area. Owens found freedom working in a middle class community, and he saw documentary opportunities that others did not. He said,

> Working for a newspaper gave me great access to the community. Doing six to ten assignments a day for the paper, I was in contact with the Chamber of Commerce, the Chief of Police, community groups, and schools. You begin to see the community from the inside out, where most people go to work all day, go home, and don't see much of their own community.[51]

Owens used his community connections to create a large project that became *Suburbia*, published in 1972. *Suburbia* showed middle-class friends and neighbors chasing the American dream with photographs, titles, and descriptions that do not mock the subjects' desires, instead they made readers feel included in the subjects' aspirations. *Suburbia* was something new in photography and it stuck a chord with audiences, leading to museums exhibits and collectors purchasing Owens' photographs. So Owens replicated success with similar themes in *Our Kind of People* (1975) and *Working (I Do It for the Money)* (1977).[52] These works were, in part, funded by a Guggenheim Fellowship and two National Endowment for the Arts scholarships.[53] Owens continued to take newspaper photographs for *The Livermore Independent* and other Bay Area newspapers throughout the 1970s. In 1980, he self-published *Publish Your Photo Book: A Guide to Self Publishing*.

Soon after, Bill was fired from *The Livermore Independent* and his first wife, Janet, took their two sons and left him. He felt that he had exhausted his photography career and was ready for something else. Owens said, "beer's expensive so I was brewing my own beer."[54] Fortunately, he had been homebrewing for 11 years and found himself with "plenty of time to brew."[55] After experimenting with homemade brewing equipment Owens decided to open a micro-brewery in 1981. He attended workshops offered by Dr. Lewis at UC Davis and professional brewing conferences. He read the stapled copies of *Amateur Brewer, Home Fermenter's Digest*, and other brewing materials available at the local homebrew shop in San Leandro. He noticed that the recipes and advice were often redundant and focused on ingredients, not materials, and that most brewing news focused on the rise of small, independent, and traditional breweries through the late 1970s and early 1980s. Owens merged his publishing and homebrewing experiences by self-publishing *How to Build a Small Brewery: Draft Beer in Ten Days* in 1982.

How to Build a Small Brewery was initially distributed through homebrew and wine-making shops alongside works by Eckhardt, Coe, Burch, Papazian, and others, and was revised and expanded in a second edition with numerous drawings and photographs in 1989 and again in 1992. Owens sold over 30,000 copies of the first two editions by 1992, and has continued selling copies since.[56] It was the first work to focus on building an all-grain brewery at home by using commonly available materials such as picnic igloos, kegs, water heaters, and garden hoses. While Owens did not create the innovative ideas, he pulled them from different sources and put them together in one innovative package.

Prior to *How to Build a Small Brewery*, most homebrewers brewed with malt extract, a thick, sugary syrup made from malted barley that was widely available in homebrew shops and grocery stores. A homebrewer would create wort by boiling the malt extract with water and hops for a set amount of time depending on the desired beer style. Once the wort is cooled it is transferred to a fermenting vessel, often a five-gallon glass carboy or plastic bucket, where the yeast is added. In the late 1970s there were few choices of malt extract types, and many already had generic hop flavor. As the interest in homebrew picked up, diverse malt extracts came on the market. Homebrew shops also supplied specialty malts and grains to add a little bit of color or different flavor to a homebrew on top of the malt extract. There are hundreds of malted grain varieties that are used in various ways and can be grouped in various categories (e.g., by process, enzymatic activity, color of wort, expected flavor).[57] With the introduction of *How to Build a Small Brewery*, many homebrewers switched from extract brewing to all-grain brewing, purchasing base malts in lieu of extract and adding portions of specialty malts, giving more control to the brewing process and mirroring large brewery practices. The best part of Owens' system is that it works by gravity, limiting the amount of physical effort required.

Owens experimented with different homemade setups for mashing, or using hot water to extract sugars from malted grain to create wort. Mashing takes place in a mash tun, a vessel that keeps malt and hot water at a consistent temperature and allows the resultant wort to be separated from the spent grain.[58] One of Owens' innovations was the igloo mash tun with a false bottom or way of filtering the wort from the grain. Bill Owens said,

> [I]n those days most guys would mash in the oven overnight. You put the mash in the water in the oven and close the door, and then you heat up to 152 [degrees], and you'd hold it overnight to get starch conversion. So I was very interested in how starch conversion was taking place. And you couldn't go to a big [brewery] on a tour and figure out what the hell was going on in a mash tun because they didn't show that. Nobody in the public's interested in that.[59]

From Dr. Lewis's workshop and thorough research, Owens found that 152 degrees was the optimal temperature for starch conversion, where the heat activates enzymes in the malted barley to change starches into sugars. Fortunately, camping coolers used by work trucks, and readily available at hardware stores, could hold water and grain at that temperature for a few hours. Owens initially used a coiled tube with holes cut in it as the false bottom, allowing the hot wort to drain and leave the grain behind (see figure 1). He found that the holes quickly got blocked, so he took a hacksaw and cut small slots in copper pipes fitted to the drain hole. Because the igloo mash tun was safer than leaving the oven on overnight, easier to use with readily-available materials, easier to clean up, and more efficient, it was quickly adopted throughout the homebrew community. When Owens was writing the first edition of the book, he documented his homebrewing process.

The homebrew setup in figures 1 through 6 was in Bill Owens' garage in Livermore, California. Figure 1 shows an early attempt at the false bottom. Figure 2 shows cracked malted barley being sparged, or the grain being rinsed with hot water to extract as much sugar as possible.[60] Owens used another piece of slotted copper pipe to slowly disperse the hot water. Cracked malted barley increases the surface area in contact with the water, but leaves the grain large enough to act as its own filter. Figure 3 shows the converted keg kettle serving as a hot liquor source. Owens gave detailed instructions on how to cut a commercial beer keg and add plumbing in the bottom so the keg kettle can serve double duty: to create hot liquor (water before mixing with grain) and to boil wort with hops. Not shown is the wort transferring from the igloo mash tun into a bucket then into the keg kettle. The wort is boiled in the keg kettle for a set amount of time, typically 60 minutes.

Specific types and amounts of hops are added in intervals, depending on the recipe. A variety of oils and chemical compounds in hops provide the bitterness and aroma to beer. The bitterness retards the growth of unwanted bacteria and yeast in the beer, thus lengthening shelf time of the final product. The flavors and bitterness of the beer vary based on the type, amount, and timing of hops used, and the intended beer style.[61] Once finished, the hopped wort is transferred to the fermenting vessel. An old adage goes "brewers make wort, yeast makes beer." Because hot sugar water is very attractive to airborne yeast and bacteria, brewers must quickly cool down the wort to fermentation temperature.

The second big innovation of *How to Build a Small Brewery* is the garden hose heat exchanger, as seen in figure 4. This "tube in shell" system is a copper tube inside of a common garden hose. The hot wort runs through the copper tube and cold water runs around the copper in the hose. This system can cool 10 gallons of wort to a usable temperature in about 30 minutes without exposing it to unwanted contamination.[62] Figure 4 shows the wort going from keg kettle, through the garden hose wort chiller, and into the five-gallon glass carboy where the yeast will be added and controlled fermentation will take place. Generic brewer's lager and ale yeast were all that was available in the late 1970s and early 1980s, though now there are hundreds of yeast strains available to homebrewers and professional brewers alike. The brewer's yeast strains are separated into seven broad categories based on desired fermenting outcomes, and are used alongside wild, once-undesirable strains that have now been "tamed."[63] Since cascade hop pellets were ubiquitous in early craft beers from Anchor, New Albion, Sierra Nevada, and others, they became the flavor and aroma of "good beer." Homebrewers sought out this specific hop variety to recreate the new craft beer styles.[64]

Figure 6 shows yeast happily fermenting (as brewers say), converting the sugars in the wort and producing flavor compounds, carbon dioxide, and ethanol (base alcohol). Owens used two five-gallon glass carboys with a water-filled airlock on the left and a blow-off tube on the right. These devices prevent airborne bacteria from interrupting the yeast at work while allowing carbon dioxide to escape, preventing a literal blow-up of foamy, yeasty, sticky liquid. The converted mini-fridge allows for temperature control. Glass carboys allow the brewer to watch yeast activity. The timing of yeast completing their work depends on the type and health of the yeast, amount of sugar in the wort, ambient temperature, and other factors. Owens suggests fermenting at 70 degrees or room temperature using ale yeast (ale yeast happily ferments at warmer temperatures while lager yeast want cooler temperatures). Once yeast activity stops, the brewer transfers the beer away from the trub—the yeast, malt proteins, and hop material that settles to the bottom of the fermenter. The brewer may transfer the beer to a keg or bottles, or may transfer to a secondary fermenter for lagering—the German term for "storing." Beer is lagered for several weeks at or near freezing temperatures so that yeast-derived flavor compounds are scrubbed from the beer, leaving a "crisp and clean taste."[65] Since Owens' book was about expediency to obtain fresh beer, he recommends leaving the beer on the yeast and turning the fridge down to 32 degrees for a few days until the beer clears, then transfer to a keg, prime it with carbon dioxide, and connect it to a picnic tap. In ten days, the homebrewer will have fresh beer.[66]

This innovation was revolutionary for amateur and would-be professional brewers. Charlie Papazian said, "He did well with it. Got people thinking."[67] Brendan Moylan bought the first edition and immediately switched from extract brewing to all-grain brewing. His successes at homebrewing using Owens' system directly led him to open two award-winning brewpubs—Marin Brewing Company in Larkspur, California in 1989 and Moylan's Brewing Company in Novato, California in 1994.[68] Tony Magee of Lagunitas Brewing Company and Sam Calagione of Dogfish Head both referred to Owens' book as their bible when setting up their breweries.[69]

Bill Owens' how-to guide also influenced Geoff Harries' homebrewing. As he relates in the 2015 Buffalo Bill's Brewery brochure to distributors and retailers, Harries bought Owens' book in 1987 and began brewing in his garage. He was so

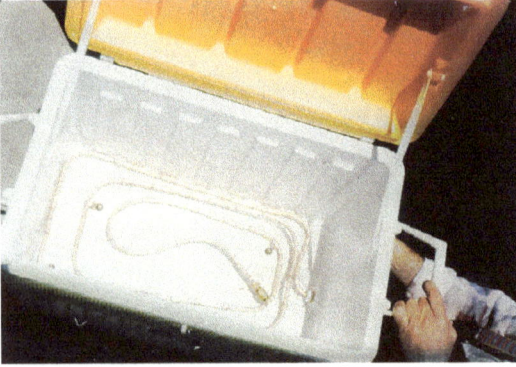

Fig 1. Bill Owens, Igloo Mash Tun
with Coiled Tube False Bottom (Early
Attempt). 1982, Color Slide. Bill Owens
Personal Archives.

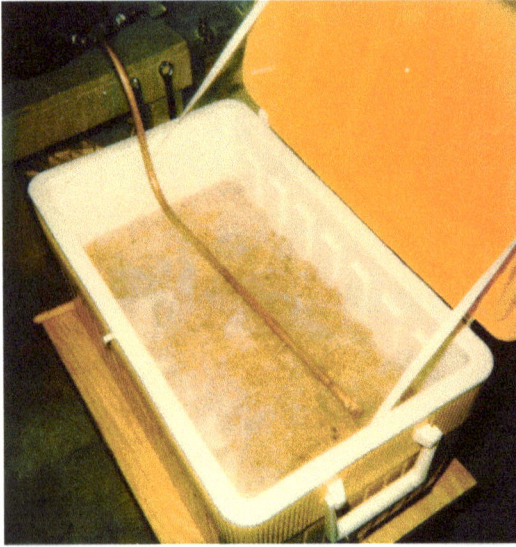

Fig 2. Bill Owens, Igloo Mash Tun with
Grain Being Sparged. 1982, Color Polaroid.
Bill Owens Personal Archives.

Fig 3. Bill Owens, Converted Keg Kettle,
Igloo Mash Tun, Water Heater Hot Liquor
Tank, Five-Gallon Glass Carboy. 1982, Color
Polaroid. Bill Owens Personal Archives.

Fig 4. Bill Owens, Wort through Garden Hose Heat Exchanger from Converted Keg Kettle to Five-Gallon Glass Carboy. 1982, Color Polaroid. Bill Owens Personal Archives.

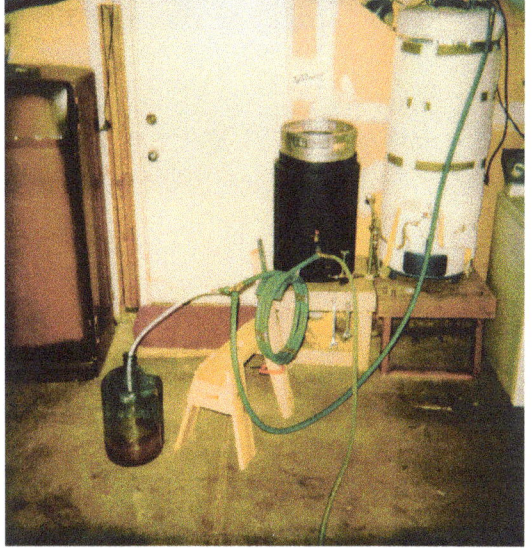

Fig 5. Bill Owens, Generic Brewer's Yeast and Cascade Hops Pellets. October 1982, Color Slide. Bill Owens Personal Archives.

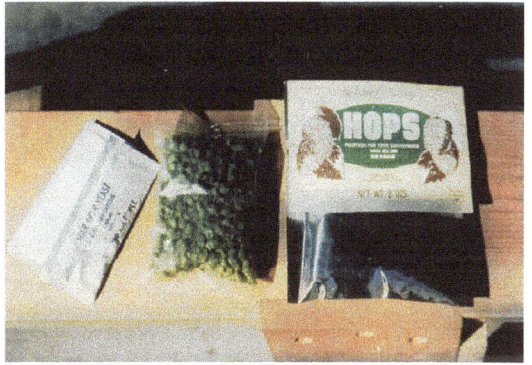

Fig 6. Bill Owens, Two Five-Gallon Glass Carboys of Beer Pitched with Yeast, One with Airlock and One with Blow-Off Tube, in a Converted Mini-Fridge. October 1982, Color Polaroid. Bill Owens Personal Archives.

inspired by Owens' work that he walked into Buffalo Bill's Brewery and asked for a job.[70] Bill Owens said no, but asked if he was willing to work for free. Harries worked for Owens for seven years before purchasing Buffalo Bill's Brewery and running it to this day. While working at Buffalo Bill's, Owens and Harries completely revised *How to Build a Small Brewery* and added new pictures and illustrations.[71] Even if no one else purchased a copy of the book, Owens' legacy was assured through Harries purchase of the book leading to the purchase of the brewpub.

Bill Owens had the idea for a micro-brewery in 1981, spent over a year researching, testing recipes, and writing *How to Build a Small Brewery*, when three opportunities came along to change his plans. The first event was when Bert Grant, a brewing industry veteran, incorporated the Yakima Brewing and Malting Company Yakima, Washington in December, 1981.[72] When it opened early 1982, Yakima Brewing was the first brewpub in the United States since Prohibition by serving beer in a brewery-owned pub next to the brewery. As Dick Cantwell says, "The brewpub is a modern business model for an ancient practical concept: serving and selling beer on the premises where it is brewed."[73] At the time the three-tier system was still firmly in place, so producers such as a brewery could not legally sell their product directly to consumers. Grant did not care, nor was he bothered by the Department of Alcohol, Tobacco, and Firearms. Bill Owens dismissed Grant's claim to being the first brewpub because Grant kegged the beer and rolled it into the adjoining bar, effectively self-distributing the beer to himself.[74] But, now that there was one brewpub in the country, there would be more.

The second event that shifted Owens' focus was a presentation about brewpubs by David Bruce, owner of the Firkin chain of brewpubs in the United Kingdom, at the Association of Brewers Conference in June, 1982. Charlie Papazian remembers that Bill "thought that was a great idea."[75] Bruce purchased flagging pubs and added small, primitive brewing equipment, creating the first modern brewpub chain. The big draw for customers was seeing, smelling, and hearing the beer being made.[76] The brewpub concept fulfilled Owens' desire for fresh beer.

The third event was an ongoing debate about legalizing brewpubs in California. Assemblyman Tom Bates who had authored the homebrewing law was interested in promoting the growing micro-brewery industry, especially for his constituents in Alameda County, as there were numerous micro-breweries in the area. Bates had served in the Army in Germany in the mid-1960s, where, he said, he was exposed to "really good beer."[77] Though he was friends with homebrewers and micro-brewers, he was not a brewer. After consulting with Dr. Lewis at UC Davis and numerous brewers and would-be brewers, Bates wrote California Assembly Bill 3610, which allowed brewers to sell directly to consumers. At this point, Bill Owens was so invested in the brewpub idea that he testified in its favor during committee hearings at the California Assembly and Se nate. Large breweries saw direct sales as a threat to their business but when Bates amended the bill to require brewpubs to service food alongside beer opposition vanished.[78] Governor Jerry Brown signed AB 3610 into law on September 13, 1982, and went into effect January 1, 1983, beginning the race for the first legal brewpub in the US.

Owens knew he had a few months to get his business in place. When he asked how to money his CPA pulled out a Limited Partnership Agreement form and whited out "almond farm" and put in "brewery."[79] Owens wrote a prospectus for potential investors in July 1982, explaining the concept of a brew pub to be opened in Hayward, California. Since it was such a new concept, the terms "brew pub," "brewpub," "brewery," and "micro-brewery" were used interchangeably. The location was set and the schedule of brewing 100 gallons every Monday, fermenting for seven days, then lagering (aging) for 21 days was in place. Owens was seeking 25 partners at $2,500 each for $62,500 to build out the first California brewpub, for which did not yet have a name. The anticipated benefits of partnership included:

- Participation in the first Brew Pub built in the San Francisco Bay Area.
- The Brew Pub is designed after the highly successful English Brew Pubs.
- Chain, Franchise potential.
- The Brew Pub has economical [*sic*] feasibility. The potential for quick cash distribution. Minimum on investment before general partner shares in profits.
- Some investment tax credits.[80]

The anticipated opening date was March 1983. Owens contemplated two locations, Walnut Creek and Hayward, but settled on downtown Hayward because of the cost—the rent was cheaper ($2,000 a month), and he could move to a house within walking distance of work. Owens eventually raised $92,000 at $3,000 per share.[81] He recorded the business name as California Brew Pub, Limited at the Alameda County Recorder's Office on January 12, 1983.[82] The next day he filed for a license at the California Department of Alcohol Beverage Control and a week later signed the lease in downtown Hayward. Owens then applied for the business license, a Federal Identification Number, a use permit, and building permits including electrical, plumbing, and mechanical.[83] All was going well with the construction on

Fig 7. Bill Owens, The Buffalo and Bill with Beer in BBB Before Opening. 1983, Black and White Photo. Bill Owens Personal Archives.

the property until an employee argued with the building inspector, leading to a failed inspection and a stalling of the process. The employee was fired before the brewpub was even open, but eventually it passed the inspection.

Buffalo Bill's Brewery opened on September 9, 1983. Unbeknownst to Owens, the Hopland Brewery, Tavern, Beer Garden, and Restaurant opened in August 1983 in Hopland, California, 120 miles north of Hayward. Hopland, now called Mendocino Brewing Company, beat Owens in the race to open and is officially the first brewpub in California and second in the US. It opened quickly by buying the recently decommissioned New Albion Brewing Company equipment from Jack McAuliffe and by being co-owned by the former New Albion employees including brewmaster Don Barkley.[84] Like Bert Grant at Yakima, Hopland was essentially operating as two different businesses, a brewery and a bar. While Buffalo Bill's is the third brewpub in the nation, it is the first brewpub in the US with a long draft system, drawing beer down a 62-foot line from the bright tank (storage tank under pressure) to the tap.[85]

When asked why he settled on the name Buffalo Bill's Brewery, Owens responded,

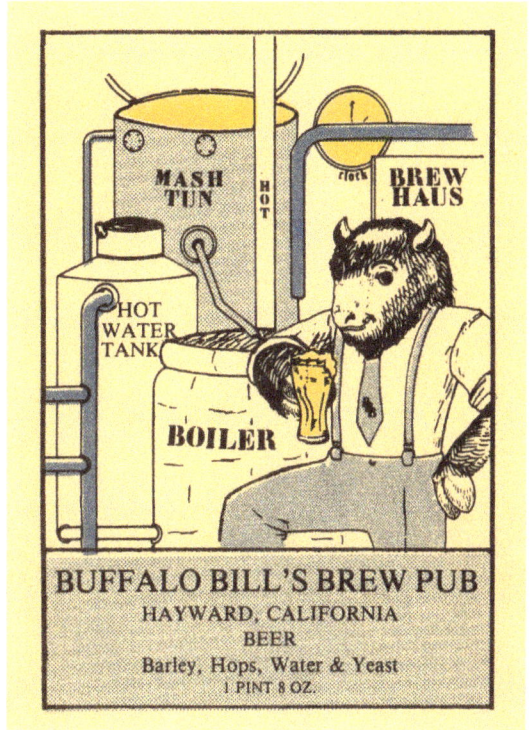

Fig 8. Bill Owens, Buffalo Bill's Brew Pub Logo for Shirts, Bottles, and Assorted Advertisements. No Date, Color Logo. Bill Owens Personal Archives.

I don't know. I wanted to name it after an American animal. I thought of the eagle and other kinds of stuff. Uhm, and I thought of Buffalo Bill's. I decided against Buffalo Bill. My name is Bill. So, I was deciding against Buffalo Bill because he killed so many Indians, and I would go with the buffalo as a natural animal. And I could buy a buffalo head to hand on the wall.[86]

Figure 7 shows Owens with the eponymous buffalo head. While Owens liked the alliteration, he did like the aspirated "p" sound in pub, preferring the softer sound of "Buffalo Bill's Brewery" to "Buffalo Bill's Brew Pub," yet both were used interchangeably at the time.[87]

The original beer lineup was a lager, an amber, and a stout, styles often available in traditional English pubs. Buffalo Brew was a lager freshly made each and every week in five barrel (155 gallon) batches using 300 pounds of grain.[88] Buffalo Amber was an ale with a dark golden to copper-brown color from additional crystal malt, barley that goes through a higher heat malting process resulting in caramelized sugars.[89] Amber ales were the number-one selling craft beer style in the US for decades.[90] Pale ales, which look similar to ambers but are much hoppier, grew more popular than ambers in the early 2000s only to be overtaken in 2011 by India Pale Ales (IPAs), which are even hoppier.[91] Owens gets credit for naming amber ale despite amber malt extract having existed for decades in part because Owens promoted his beers by their colors. He felt that customers knew they wanted fresh beer but would not know different styles, so he wanted to "play all the colors."[92] Mosher quotes Bill as saying, "I had a dark and a light, and what was I gonna call that middle one? Amber."[93] Buffalo Stout was a traditional stout with roasted specialty grains, marking the dark end of the spectrum. Other beers on tap were quality import and micro-brewed beers including Spaten, Watneys, Guinness, Heineken, Sierra Nevada, and St. Stan's.

Brian Hunt, owner and brewer at Moonlight Brewery, argued that small brewers brewed English style beers like pale ales, porters, and stouts because they read English-language homebrewing books. Hunt said about Owens, "He was not a good follower, He was not a good sheep. [...] Thank God Bill was crazy and irreverent. The world was a better place because of him."[94] While Hunt, a graduate of Dr. Lewis' program at UC Davis and a veteran brewer, helped Owens figure out how to make his assemblage of equipment do what Owens wanted, he was not enamored with Buffalo Bill's beers. However, he said, "It was revolutionary. No one had made beer that had that flavor. [...] Very few people that started the first of something did a beautiful job of it. You can't. When one tries to do something that hasn't been done, you can't exactly know what will happen."[95]

Brendan Moylan echoed the sentiment, saying Buffalo Bill's was one of his favorite places to hang out because of the freshness of the beer.[96] Moylan first stepped into Buffalo Bill's as a beer distributor delivering kegs of Spaten for the brewpub's opening. Owens remembers Moylan as having explained to him glycol systems, how to keep beer cold down that 62-foot draft line so it does not pour foam.[97] Owens said Moylan "saved his hide", but Moylan does not remember the conversation.[98] They both agree that when Moylan first entered Buffalo Bill's he said "I want to do this!" Owens offered six-minute tours of the brewhouse to anyone who asked. Figure 8 shows the original brewery logo with the brewhouse prominently displayed. This logo was used in print advertisements, on t-shirts, and on upcoming bottled beer. Figure 12 is an early design for the brewhouse use to explain the brew process for potential investors. Figures 14 and 15 are the proposed floorplans and detailed brewhouse layout.

Despite enthusiastically sharing the brewing process in detail, Owens continued to market the beers by color. Moylan felt it was important to educate consumers, thus at Marin Brewing Company he handwrote 3x5 card descriptions of the beers and their alcohol by volume to be displayed at the brewpub and on retail shelves. He said, "[I was] one of the original beer nerds, trying to educate drinkers at the point of sales."[99] Hunt and Moylan agree with Owens that consumers were looking for something new and fresh, and they eagerly drank it up.

As the first brewpub in the US serving directly from the draft line, Owens helped set the expectation for all other brewpubs. His food option (required by law) was limited because Buffalo Bill's did not have a stove. The pub offered soup and sandwiches for lunch, with occasional pizzas, with materials bought at Price Club (now Costco).[100] In the evening, as customers arrived after work, the kitchen closed and the place became a bar, serving beer and bagged chips. Owens proudly claims to be the first person to ban smoking in the bar in the mid-1980s. He was tired of

[Top] Fig 9. Bill Owens. Buffalo Bill's Brewery in 1983. 1983, Color Photograph. Bill Owens Personal Archives.

[Bottom] Fig 10. Bill Owens. Buffalo Bill's Brewery First Makeover. No Date, Color Photograph. Bill Owens Personal Archives.

Fig 11. Bill Owens. Triptych of Happy Customers. No Date, Black and White Photographs. Bill Owens Personal Archives.

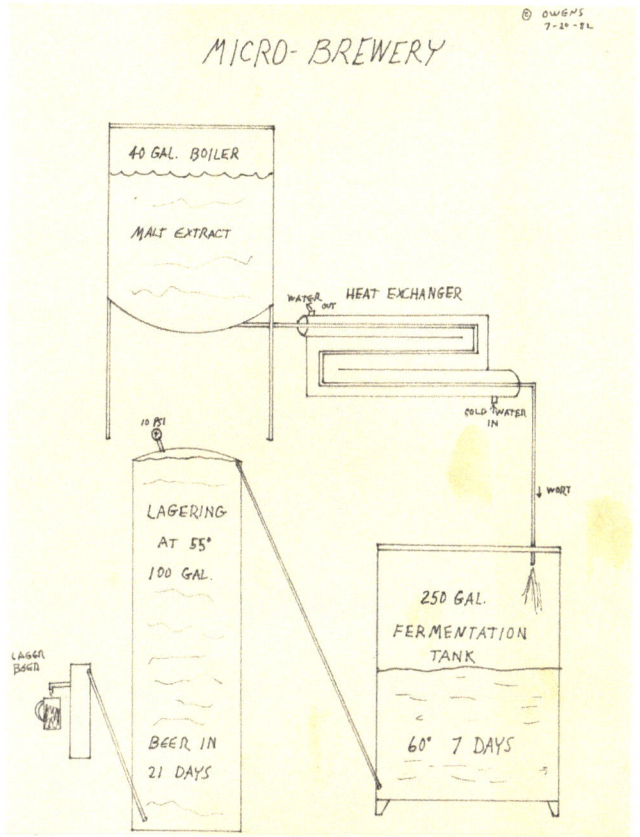

[Top] Fig 12. Bill Owens. Micro-Brewery Drawn for Prospective Investors. July 20, 1982, Pen on Cardstock. Bill Owens Personal Archives.

[Bottom] Fig 13. Bill Owens. Bill at the Threshold of Brewery and Pub. 1983, Black and White Photograph. Bill Owens Personal Archives.

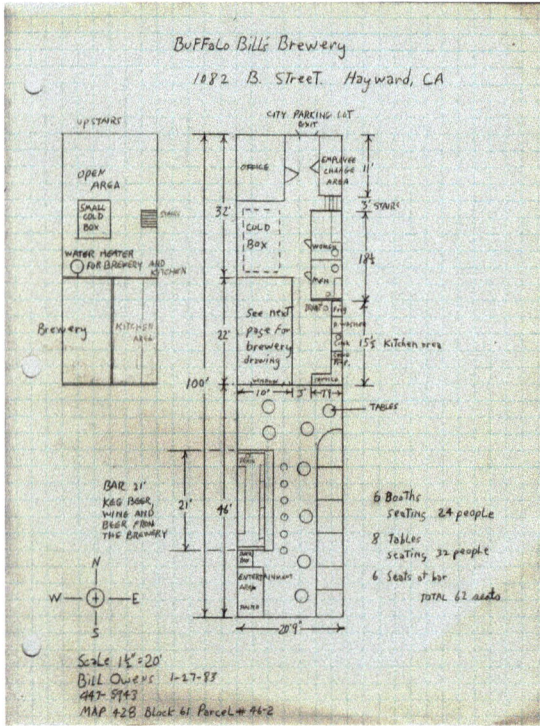

[Top] Fig 14. Bill Owens, Buffalo Bill's Brewery Floor Plans. January 27, 1983, Pencil on Graph Paper. Bill Owens Personal Archives.

[Bottom] Fig 15. Bill Owens. Buffalo Bill's Brewery Brewhouse and Instructions. January 27, 1983, Pencil on Graph Paper. Bill Owens Personal Archives.

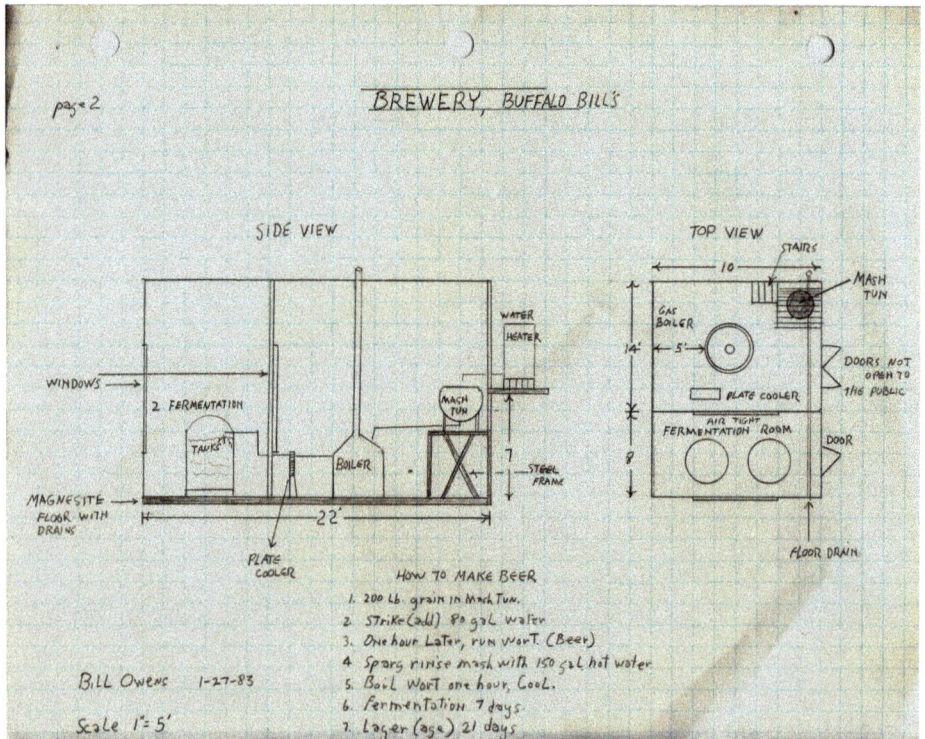

Fig 16. Bill Owens. Bill in the Brewhaus Stirring the Kettle, for the Tourists. No Date, Color Photograph. Bill Owens Personal Archives.

the lingering smell of cigarette smoke, cigarette butts littering the floor, and nicotine residue staining the glass windows and mirrors.[101] While Buffalo Bill's was not quite like the family-friendly restaurant breweries that came later (as seen in figures 9 and 10), it was more comfortable than the average bar, with darts, a pool table, and a view of the brewery to keep customers entertained (as seen in figures 11 and 16).

Buffalo Bill's Brewery opened with a bang, literally. Bill Owens arranged for a saxophonist to play the William Tell Overture while local Civil War reenactors in full regalia shot off a cannon on B Street in downtown Hayward. Owens warned his neighboring businesses of the impending noise, but they were not concerned as they would be closed by 6pm on Saturday. Owens said,

> So we just waited till the traffic light turned, so there'd be no traffic in front of it. Then we did "duh-duh-duh, duh-duh-duh, BOOM!" And the smoke… first off, it was like a stick of dynamite. Your clothes shook, we were in total shock of the noise. The smoke rolled across the street, blocked out the, good thing there was no traffic, you couldn't've seen anything. And it kicked off the alarm at the bank, so the police department showed up. (laughs)[102]

Though the brewpub was small at 2,075 square feet it made quite an impact on the local community (figures 21-23). The cannoneers and saxophones returned every anniversary. The beer cost $0.07 per glass to make, and sold for $1.50. Because of its position as one of the first brewpubs, and because of his experience as a photojournalist, Owens was featured in numerous magazines are newspaper articles. A nine-page cover article about the burgeoning craft beer movement in The Atlantic Monthly quoted Owens as saying, "[t]he wave is the brew pub, and I'm on the crest."[103] Owens later said,

> My fun is promoting. If the television camera is here, I get out my big paddle and stir the mash. It's not necessary to stir. It's just graphic. I'm not the edge of the revolution—the making-money-and-enjoying-it revolution. A lot of microbrewers are purists. Ale is the Holy Grail. I'm not interested in that. You find chemists and chefs—I'm a chef. I know my truth is best. I do it the easy way. […] You can't have it your way. You get it my way. […] The style brings a customer in, but it's the beer that has to bring him back.[104]

Owens was not wrong about customers returning, particularly as he expanded his lineup of beers, and changed the way breweries experiment with beer styles.

Bill Owens initially wanted to offer customers beer in a range of colors with an emphasis on freshness. While brewing 450 barrels a year and running a business, Owens actively promoted Buffalo Bill's Brewery wherever and whenever he could. He also stayed connected to the large microbrewery industry by continually attending Master Brewers Association of the Americas presentations, presenting at Association of Brewers conferences (now Brewers Association), and participating in the Great American Beer Festival in Colorado. In 1985, after reading how President George Washington brewed beer using a variety of vegetables including pumpkins and gourds at Mount Vernon, Owens decided to expand his beer lineup with a one-off, a beer recipe that is intended to be made only once. This limited edition beer was called Punkin' Ale. He grew a 65-pound giant pumpkin in his yard, hauled it to Buffalo Bill's in the back of his truck with a cargo net over it, chopped it up, baked it, and threw it in the mash tun with his regular amber ale malt (as seen in figure 17). After running the mash, Owens brewed the beer just like the Buffalo Amber. After fermentation was complete, he explained,

Fig 17. Bill Owens, Pumpkin Roasted and Pumpkin Mashed. No Date, Color Photograph. Bill Owens Personal Archives.

you can taste, well, there is no pumpkin flavor. Sorry. So, uh, you're scratching your head on what the hell to do, so you just walk into, at that time right across the street was a supermarket, a Lucky's. And you just walk into Lucky's to the shelf that said "pumpkin pie spices," go to the coffee percolator, pour in the whole can of spices, and percolate up about a quart of it. And then you go back to the five-barrel fermentation tank, pour it in, carbonate, and then go on to the bar. So anybody tells you they're not adding spices is lying to you, cuz [sic] you can't get a cinnamon taste, a pumpkin is a gourd! There is no flavor, in a gourd. Not your pumpkin pie flavor.[105]

Punkin' Ale was Buffalo Bill's first bottled beer, hand-bottled in 24-ounce champagne bottles. It was sold for $3.50 at the brewpub and through the mail.[106] Owens said he used that size bottle because the weird-sized glass was cheaper and it was less labor-intensive than bottling and labeling 12 ounce bottles.[107] Punkin' Ale sold out for its sheer novelty. It was one of the first seasonal beers, being released in autumn, and is the first commercial pumpkin ale.[108] Though pumpkin does not add substantial amounts of sugar or flavor to beers, pumpkin ales have become big business for craft brewers and large brewers alike.[109] Dick Cantwell, former brewer and owner of Elysian Brewery in Seattle, Washington, created the annual Great Pumpkin Beer Festival in 2004. At the 2015 event, Elysian brewed 15 different pumpkin beers, and 50 other breweries brought at least one beer.[110] These beers varied in style, brewing process, and additional spices and flavors added to beer, from coffee to peach. Buffalo Bill's now offers three versions of pumpkin beer: America's Original Pumpkin Ale, Black Pumpkin Oatmeal Stout, and Imperial Pumpkin Ale (9.8% alcohol by volume (ABV) compared to the original's 6%).

Due to demand among consumers, what once was a Halloween special was released in September, then August, and now July. This "seasonal drift" affects other seasonal beers with it. Cold weather, spiced Christmas ales are released in October; marzens (named after the German word for March, when they are traditional available) come out in January; light, refreshing summer ales are now released in rainy April.[111] But, as Bart Watson, chief economist for the Brewers Association, noted, interest in pumpkin ales wanes by Halloween yet Christmas beers' popularity begins at Thanksgiving. So, seasonal drift has created an opportunity to release special beers in November between the two seasonal beer juggernauts.[112] Owens' experiment in brewing a historical recreation altered the brewing landscape. To increase his publicity, Owens advertised in beer publications and mentioned in every interview that he sold seeds for giant pumpkin and the famous recipe through the mail. Owens admitted that only two or three people ever took him up on the offer, and he mailed them a few seeds from the home garden store, but selling the seeds drew attention to the beer. "My entrepreneurial spirit was quite strong," he laughed.[113] Owens placed all spent grain in buckets in the alley for a local farmer to collect weekly and feed to his pigs. The farmer noted that the pigs especially enjoyed the roast pumpkin. Owens continued to grow the pumpkins in his yard in Hayward, California, for the annual batch of Pumpkin Ale. (see figure 20.)

In 1985, after Owens' CPA went through a divorce, Bill sought to create the bitterest beer in America and named it Alimony Ale. To achieve the high bitterness, Owens tripled the amount of hops he used in Buffalo Amber from three ounces of Cascade hop pellets to nine ounces per five barrels. This created a beer that was 50 IBUs (International Bitterness Units) compared to the standard 20-25 IBUs of pale ales at the time.[114] Owens arguably created the first American India Pale Ale by focusing on hoppiness. IPAs are the number one selling craft beer in the US, followed by seasonal beers including pumpkin ales.[115] Owens followed Alimony Ale with Hearty Ale, an Imperial IPA brewed in honor of Buffalo Bill's bartender who survived heart surgery.[116]

Hearty Ale was one of the first Imperial or Double IPAs, a beer style name that would not be coined for another decade. The term imperial or double refers to a recipe that has higher levels of hops and malt than the regular version of the beer style, leading to a stronger or higher alcohol style.[117] Finally, in 1985, Owens received a mysterious package in the mail, three small cans, each about the size of peanut cans and stuffed with hop pellets from Tasmania. So he brewed an imperial version of Buffalo Amber with only Tasmanian hops and called it Tasmanian Devil with an image of the marsupial on the logo.[118] Owens was the first US brewer to make an Australian-hopped beer, leading to more publicity. Unfortunately, that press got the attention of Warner Bros., who threatened to sue Buffalo Bill's Brewery for trademark infringement of the Looney Tunes character. Owens was deposed in Los Angeles and swore under oath that he was not inspired to create a beer by a cartoon. Though Warner Bros. did not pursue a lawsuit this controversy created more publicity for Buffalo Bill's Brewery.

All four products (Pumpkin Ale, Alimony Ale, Hearty Ale, and Tasmanian Devil) were bottled by hand at Buffalo Bill's Brewery with priming sugar, a labor-intensive process (see figure 19 for an example of hand-filling beer). Over time, Owens introduced other seasonal and one-off beers including wits or spiced Belgian wheat ales, Octoberfests, brown ales, Christmas ales, Russian imperial stouts, and barleywines.[119] Figure 18 shows various labels used over the years.[120] Buffalo Bill's small size and constant consumer demand allowed Owens to continually experiment with beer styles and recipes.

Though Owens developed Buffalo Bill's recipes himself, he was not brewing alone. Younger men, mostly homebrewers, visited Buffalo Bill's Brewery looking to break into the industry. Owens would teach them the recipes and set them to work as seen in figure 19. Many of those brewers went on to work at breweries and distilleries around the country, including Geoff Harries, the future owner of Buffalo Bill's Brewery

Fig 18. Geoff Harries. Montage of Labels, 1985-2015. "Buffalo Bill's Brewery 2015," Buffalo Bill's Brewery, 2015.

[Top] Fig 19. Bill Owens, Unnamed Assistant Brewer Hand-Filling Pumpkin Ale. No Date, Color Photograph. Bill Owens Personal Archives.

[Bottom} Fig 20. Bill Owens, Bill and Hand-grown, Handpicked Pumpkins, for the Beer. No Date, Color Photograph. Bill Owens Personal Archives.

Fig 21. Bill Owens, Buffalo Bill's Brewery with Brewhouse behind the Glass, Buffalo behind the Bar, and Beer in Drinkers' Hands. No Date, Color Photograph. Bill Owens Personal Archives.

Fig 22. Bill Owens. A Bouquet of Various Tap Handles. No Date, Black and White Photographs. Bill Owens Personal Archives.

[Top] Fig 23. Bill Owens, *Celebrating Another Year of Buffalo Bill's with a Boom.* September, 1985, Black and White Photograph. Bill Owens Personal Archives.

[Bottom] Fig 24. Bill Owens, *Interior Sign, In Case One Forgets Where They Are.* No Date, Color Photograph. Bill Owens Personal Archives.

[Left] Fig 26. Bill Owens, Bison Brewery: At the Corner of Telegraph and Parker. No Date, Color Polaroid. Bill Owens Personal Archives

[Above] Fig 27. Bill Owens, Bison Brewery in Fall. No Date, Color Photograph. Bill Owens Personal Archives.

Fig 25. Bill Owens, Brewpub on the Green. No Date, Color Polaroid. Bill Owens Personal Archives.

CHAPTER THREE
Spreading the Love, 1985-1997

Although bottled beers were successful, they had lower profit margins than draft beer because of labor and material costs. In 1986, Bill Owens found a way to profitably bottle beer through contract brewing. Contract brewing can vary by agreement but typically one brewery does the brewing and bottling for another brewery.[121] Owens worked with a variety of contract brewers through the years, including August Shell Brewing, Dubuque Brewing, Portland Brewing, and Pyramid Brewery.[122] While Owens was brewing five-barrel batches of beer each week, the contract brewer could fill a 32-foot truck with 50 barrels of packaged beer. They delivered it to wholesalers, who distributed it to retailers, who sold it to customers. Owens would pay out of pocket about $11,000 for the truckload, and would receive a check six months later for his money back plus profit.[123] Bottles of Alimony Ale, Pumpkin Beer, and Billy Bock (a spring seasonal) were sold across the country and continued to draw national attention to Buffalo Bill's Brewery.

Running a successful brewpub and a successful contract brewing company are two full-time jobs. When Geoff Harries, the twenty-year-old homebrewer who relied on Owens' *How to Build a Small Brewery*, met Bill Owens in 1987 he was denied a job but offered an opportunity to work for free. Harries became a permanent assistant brewer at Buffalo Bill's, allowing Bill to focus on other ventures. Inspired by David Bruce's presentation in 1982, and as indicated on the prospectus to investors, Owens intended to franchise the brewpub idea. In the Fall 1986 issue of *American Brewer: The Micro-Brewer/Brew Pub Magazine*, Owens declared that he applied and received trademark protection of "brewpub" in California in summer 1985 and applied for federal protection on August 8, 1985. His goal was to protect Buffalo Bill's and future franchises' model of micro pub breweries. He intended to license the term "brewpub" on a sliding scale to individuals who wanted to replicate his business plan.[124] Brendan Moylan recalls that Owens wanted to protect the trademark so large companies would not take advantage of small brewers, and that Owens never harassed anyone who used the term.[125] The craft beer industry was known for its collegiality as established by Maytag, McAuliffe, Grossman, et al. The idea of a craft brewer quashing competition rankled a few people in the small community. Owens admits that it was a "harebrained story" so he dropped it.[126] But he did not give up on the idea of franchising brewpubs.

With Geoff Harries in place at Buffalo Bill's Brewery, Owens focused on opening Brewpub on the Green in Fremont, south of Hayward. Owens used the same limited partnership structure and business plan to find investors. Initially called Central Park Café and Brewery before opening in 1988, Brewpub on the Green was a large brewpub next to a golf course with a full kitchen and ten-barrel brewhouse, double the capacity of Buffalo Bill's Brewery. Harries brewed beer at Buffalo Bill's on Mondays and at Brewpub on the Green on Tuesdays.[127] Though he used the same recipes as at Buffalo Bill's, he had to recalibrate them because of the larger system.[128] The general manager was a friend of Owens' CPA, and he let Brewpub on the Green fall into disarray and was not paying bills, continually pulling Owens' time and attention to the second brewpub. After firing the manager, Harries became the resident general manager and brewer in Fremont, and Brewpub on the Green was successful. In 1991,

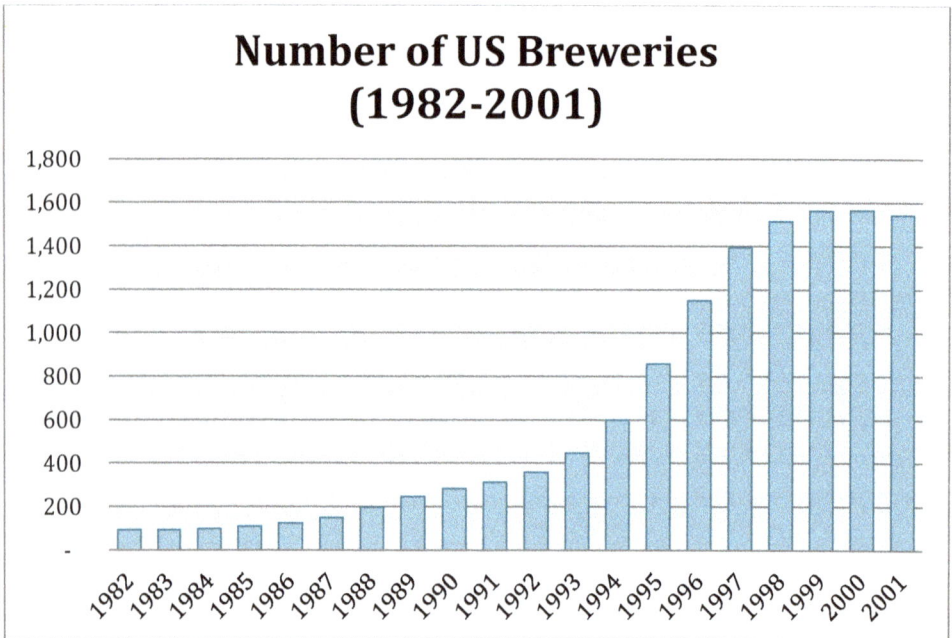

Number of US Breweries (1982-2001)

Fig 28. Number of US Breweries (1982-2001). Data from Brewers Association.

the landlord gave Owens a $170,000 bill for parking lot fees and other unpaid fees (due to the previous manager), causing Bill to wash his hands of the brewpub. He sold it for almost no profit, just enough to pay off the debts on it.[129] It continued to run for fewer than two years before being torn down and turned into residential housing.

Before Harries took over at Brewpub on the Green (and before poor management caused problems), Bill Owens focused on the third franchise. Using the same structure and plan, Owens raised $300,000 for Bison Brewery in Berkeley, north of Hayward. Bison, the third brewpub in Berkeley, opened in 1989. David Baker, the architect, designed the building with a two-story glass window in the front, and hand-made light fixtures and terrazzo tiles (see figures 26 and 27).[130] Owens said the décor was "between Italian 'boldism' and Pee Wee Herman; lots of fun."[131] The 15-barrel brewpub (triple Buffalo Bill's capacity) opened with a general manager and 15 employees. Within a month the manager and half the employees were fired—Bison was not making money. Soon, Owens became manager and ran the place with three employees.[132] Despite the beautiful building in a great location near UC Berkeley, the full kitchen, and the tried-and-true Buffalo Bill's fresh beer, Bison Brewery did not make money. Owens recalled that the partners would call business meetings in a panic, and he used money from Buffalo Bill's to pay debts at Bison. He explained "you can only do so many meetings and then, they want you gone."[133] Owens walked away from Bison Brewery a year after it opened. While he did not lose money, he gained freedom to pursue other ventures. He also learned that, though a business plan may be replicated, success may not follow.

Bison Brewery went through a series of owners. The most recent and longest-owned group sold the building and transformed Bison into a contract brewery. In 2003, Bison became one of the first certified organic breweries in the country.[134] Bison Brewing continues Owens' innovative spirit by brewing unique beer styles such as chocolate stout, honey basil, and gingerbread ale. While numerous restaurants have occupied the building, since 2010 it has been a popular Indian/Nepali restaurant.

Even while running three brewpubs, Bill Owens wanted to open a mother brewery, a production facility to brew beer for five satellites and bottle beer for distribution. The satellites would continue brewing a signature beer, but the mother brewery would take care of seasonal and one-off products.[135] In 1989, Owens advertised for limited partnership investors to raise $2.8 million, and received no serious offers. After months of struggle, Owens shelved the mother brewery concept and tried a new business model. He incorporated Owens Brewing Company in 1990, issuing 428,571 shares of preferred stock at $2.33 per share, with the goal of raising $1 million. The company would build a micro-brewery-restaurant with 10,000-barrel brewhouse for bottling and distribution.[136] This new concept, a large-scale brewpub, was to be in Pleasanton, California, east of Hayward, but this venture also failed.[137]

Microbrewing was a booming business. According to the Brewers Association statisticians, the number of breweries grew 2 1/3 times over a ten-year period from 1982 to 1991, from 93 to 312 businesses. These numbers include New Albion Brewery, Brewpub on the Green, and numerous other breweries that did not make it, but they do not count those ventures that did not make it past the planning stage.[138] Between 1982 and 2001, 2000 saw the largest number of breweries at 1,566 as seen in figure 28. The slight dip in 2001 is accounted for breweries consolidating with both small and large breweries.

Bill Owens walked away from Bison Brewery in 1990 and sold Brewpub on the Green in 1991. In 1994 he sold Buffalo Bill's Brewery to the head brewer, Geoff Harries, but Owens retained the labels and recipes for contract brewing.[139] On the first day of ownership Harries expanded the food selection, adding pizza, bread sticks, and gourmet sandwiches and salads. In 2000, Harries expanded Buffalo Bill's into the space next door and built a patio, more than doubling the size of the brewpub.[140] Throughout the 1990s Owens continued selling Buffalo Bill's Alimony Ale and Buffalo Bill's Pumpkin Ale across the country. He said, "sales is a full-time job. You can't be running a brewery, brewpub, and doing packaging at the same time."[141] Part of the agreement with keeping the labels was that Owens would print a map to Buffalo Bill's Brewery in Hayward, California on the bottom of six-pack holders. The intent was so drinkers purchasing the beer at a store would visit the brewpub. In 1997, a shipment of older holders without the map was sent out to retailers.[142] This breach of agreement led to arbitration where Harries won a small settlement and the rights to the labels back.[143] Buffalo Bill's brewpub and contract brewing were under the same roof once more. Though Owens was out of the brewing business, he was not yet out of the brewing industry.

CHAPTER FOUR
Spreading the Word, 1985-2001

When writing *How to Build a Small Brewery* and researching his first brewery, Bill Owens pored over existing brewing materials. In the early 1980s there were some small, hand-made homebrewing newsletters with limited circulation and spotty release dates available at homebrew stores. One was *Home Fermenter's Digest*, an occasional newsletter written by the employee and girlfriend of the owner of a homebrew shop in San Leandro, California, where Owens purchased his homebrew materials. After the publication of the book and the successful opening of Buffalo Bill's Brewery, Owens still felt called to return to journalism, this time focusing on brewing. He purchased *Home Fermenter's Digest* for a small sum.[144] He then needed subscribers. Fred Eckhardt, the homebrew enthusiast and early beer writer, was having difficulty publishing *Amateur Brewer* on a regular basis, so he sold Owens his mailing list of 300-400 homebrew shops, enthusiastic homebrewers, and microbrewery industry types.[145]

Owens' first issue of his new beer magazine, the May/June 1985 issue of *Home Fermenter's Digest: The Home Brewing & Fermentation Magazine*, featured new format, new content, and a new focus on news and information from the brewing industry. As he predicted in the first issue, "we are also part of the changes going on in the industry... watch us grow."[146] The initial bi-monthly black and white magazine was aimed at home brewers and wine makers, with all of the initial ads devoted to homebrew goods. Articles were split between homebrewing help and microbrewing news. By the third issue Owens changed the name to *Amateur Brewer: The Brewing and Fermentation Magazine* then changed it again to *Amateur Brewer: The Micro-Brewer/Brew Pub™ Magazine*. It is in this issue that Owens declared to the brewing world that he held the trademark to the term brewpub.[147] The focus was continually shifting toward the brewing industry and away from homebrewing as the magazine grew in size, added larger brewery ads, color interiors, and glossy paper.

In the Fall 1986 issue Owens also publically called for Senator Alan Cranston to replicate Assemblyman Tom Bates' California AB 3610 that legalized brewpubs or direct beer sales on a national level, just as Cranston pushed Bates' homebrewing legalization in 1978.[148] Owens' magazine continued advocating for small, independent, and traditional breweries. In 1987, Owens appeared in the Congressional Record, petitioning the Bureau of Alcohol, Tobacco, and Firearms to allow brewpubs to sell beer directly to consumers nationwide.[149] In the Summer, 1988 issue of *American Brewer: The Micro-Brewer/Brewpub Magazine*, Owens responded to a letter about changing brewpub laws in West Virginia. Owens was a member of Brew-PAC (sometimes spelled BrewPAC), a political action committee working in numerous states to change pub brewing laws.[150] Owens continued proselytizing the story of craft beer whenever and wherever he could.

In the West Virginia response above, Owens used two different spellings of the PAC, something of a habit in his publications, due, in equal parts, to his dyslexia and excitement to get the information out. As he said about a later publication, "It's my magazine. I can do whatever I want with it. [...] If there are errors we can correct them later."[151] In the same manner the name of the publication changed from "amateur" to "American," then combined "brew pub" to "brewpub." For Owens, changing the title to *American Brewer* in 1987 expanded the scope on brewing on a national level.[152] The other two big magazines were published by Charlie Papazian at the Association of Brewers (now Brewers Association): *New Brewer*, focusing on the industry, and *Zymurgy*, focusing on homebrewing. Papazian recalled, "'competing' publications offered [a] different and fresh perspective. One publication couldn't [*sic*] represent all those ideas floating around at the time. That's why 'competition' emerged. It was healthy for us."[153] Since both magazines had a large organization behind them with conferences and trade shows, Owens knew his magazine needed to differentiate itself. Owens said,

> The only thing I could do with *American Brewer* was to make it better. The Writing had to be better, it had to be more interesting, and kinda be a thorn in their side to, to keep them more honest and, I mean, we went after them [...] I just always competed against them [...] with my database, my subscribers, and my followers. And I had my brewpub, with Buffalo Bill's and some interesting brands. So I attracted some pretty interesting people, you know?[154]

And so he did. Fal Allen, the brewmaster at Anderson Valley Brewing Company, explained that Owens asked him to write for *American Brewer* after reading some of his technical writing: "Bill paid me for my writing in a day when beer writers often wrote for just the love of the subject, he got me deals on brewing publications, and, as a staff writer for *American Brewer*, Bill got me many a press pass to get into events I might never had been able to get into."[155] Allen ended up having a regular column in the magazine, as did Dick Cantwell, the Pumpkin King. Cantwell's first published work in *American Brewer* was a letter pointing out that a beer he brewed at Pike Place Brewery in Seattle, Washington, Old Bawdy Barley Wine, was more bitter than Alimony Ale.[156] Instead of taking exception to the claim, Owens hired Cantwell to write articles and later a regular column. Brendan Moylan of Marin Brewing Company and Moylan Brewing Company also wrote one article about wheat beer. Moylan had an employee proofread the article then submitted it without reviewing it. Neither Moylan nor Owens noticed the technical errors in the article until it went to press.[157] Readers noticed and responded, but that only fueled Owens' engagement with his audience. With hundreds of other brewers also contributing letters, articles, recipes, and news, *American Brewer* was a nation-wide brewpub for beer fans and industry insiders alike.

In addition to showcasing brewers, *American Brewer* featured a who's who of beer writers, including Fred Eckhardt, Randy Mosher, Stan Hieronymus, Bill Metzger, and Charlie Papazian himself. Lucy Saunders wrote regular articles on food and beer pairing. She was a pioneering beer writer for both her gender and her focus on craft beer and fine food. Her book, *Cooking with Beer: Taste-Tempting Recipes and Creative Ideas for Matching Beer and Food*, was one of the first pairing guides.[158] Michael Jackson, the preeminent British beer writer who introduced the concept of beer styles in the late-1970s with *The World Guide to Beer*, regularly contributed articles about whatever beer-related item struck his fancy before he had a permanent column. *American Brewer* featured articles not just on brewers and breweries but also distributors, equipment manufacturers, hop and barley producers, breweriana (the collecting of brewery-related ephemera), recipes, trip reports, reviews, and homebrewing advice.

In 1990, Owens changed the name to *American Brewer Magazine* then to *American Brewer: The Business of Beer* in 1992, the name it still bears in 2017. Owens initially published the magazine in the back office at Buffalo Bill's Brewery and then, after selling the brewpub, from an office across the street for a year or two. The final home was in the back office of an antique store Owens purchased and ran for a few years in downtown Hayward.[159] *American Brewer* went through numerous editorial and staff changes through the years, causing its quarterly publication schedule to falter from time to time (hence issue 58 listed as "Sprung," the season between Spring and Summer), but it consistently maintained the balance of reverence and irreverence, just like the beer industry it covered.

By 1993, Bill Owens ran Buffalo Bill's Brewery, supervised contract brewing, and published *American Brewer*, which was widely recognized as a venerable quarterly trade publication with circulation of 20,000 copies.[160] Fred Dodsworth, the editor of *American Brewer*, announced that Owens Publishing would release *BEER, the magazine* [sic]. According to Dodsworth's editorial, "[t]o beer drinkers and beers lovers the world over, *BEER* promises to be the answer you have been looking for; a one source, Brew Bible and guide book to what 'ales' you."[161] A sister publication to *American Brewer*, *BEER* was an extra-large, full-colored tabloid magazine with the goal of converting the non-craft beer drinking public to "quality beers and ales produced by American brewers and imported from countries around the world."[162] Where *American Brewer* was sold through subscriptions, homebrew shops, and at breweries, *BEER: The Magazine* was also sold in bookstores, reaching a broader audience. Owens was influenced by *Wine Spectator*, his own photographic and artistic sensibilities, and his love of travel developed from Halliburton's books.[163] *BEER: The Magazine* featured stories, poetry, artwork and comic strips, recipes, travel reports, and Beerspective, a column by Michael Jackson. Many of its editorial staff and writers came over from *American Brewer* or worked at both publications. The second issue was slightly smaller, though still larger than standard magazines, and the title changed to *BeeR, the magazine* [sic], where it remained.

Although he no longer owned Alimony Ale (or maybe in spite of it), Bill Owens created the Alpha King Challenge as an unofficial event during the Great America Beer Festival (GABF) in Denver, Colorado in 1999, to crown the bitterest beer in America. *American Brewer* partnered with Nick Floyd of the eponymous Three Floyds Brewery, who brew Alpha King Pale Ale, and Ralph Olson of Hopunion, the largest vendor of fresh hops in the US (now called YCH Hops).[164] Ten beers were submitted for testing to Hopunion before the event to ensure they were at least 60 IBUs. Owens, Floyd, and Olson joined three other judges from across the beer industry in a conference room at a Holiday Inn. The judges did a blind tasting with unmarked glasses so they could not be tainted by bias. The winning beer was selected for being the best tasting, not necessarily the hoppiest. The first Alpha King Challenge winner was Two-Hearted Ale brewed by Larry Bell of Kalamazoo Brewing in Michigan (now Bell's Brewing). Owens gave Bell a $100 bill and crowned him with a crown of hops. In 2000, five new judges tasted nine beers and crowned Sockeye Red from Midnight Sun Brewing in Alaska.[165] Though 2000 was the last year that Owens participated, the Alpha King Challenge continues today. Instead of being tucked away in a Holiday Inn, it is now an official event at GABF. In 2016, Headwall Double IPA from Tamarack Brewing Co. in Lakeside, Montana won first place, topping 152 entries from 107 breweries.[166] The Alpha King Challenge continues to grow as IPAs and hoppiness dominate brewing culture.

Bill Owens was one of his biggest advertising clients in *American Brewer* and *BeeR, the magazine*. He cross-promoted both magazines, advertised Buffalo Bill's Brewery, Buffalo Bill's Alimony Ale and Pumpkin Ale, *How to Build a Small Brewery: Draft Beer in Ten Days* third edition revised in 1992, and the pumpkin seeds to make your own pumpkin ale. He also sold *BeeR, the magazine* tie-dye t-shirts, *American Brewer* metal keychain bottle openers with the phone number etched on them, and membership in The Bill Society, which earned a coat pin. The Bill Society continually offered various amounts of money for non-professional beer writers to submit their work.

Beginning in 1987, Owens periodically ran ads stating: "The Brewpub Manual. Over 100 pages on how to build and operate a brewpub: brewing process, proforma, equipment, consultants, organization, prospectus, regulations. Price: $2518.00."[167] Over time the manual was revised up to 165 pages and the price dropped down to $150.00 and then to $85.00. He also periodically advertised himself as a brewpub consultant, offering "expert/practical advise [*sic*] on: laws regulating brewpubs, brewery design, business plans, equipment manufacturers."[168] Owens said he never consulted for anyone, but he did sell a few plans, and he always offered free information and free six-minute tours at Buffalo Bill's Brewery.[169]

In 2000, Owens noted that the two organizations that normally publish annual directories of brewers and suppliers decided not to do so, so he decided to publish the *American Brewer and Distiller Directory* by compiling information and using industry contacts from 15 years of publishing.[170] The addition of craft distillers reflected a growing awareness in the burgeoning craft spirits movement, particularly since they use many of the same base ingredients, equipment, and procedures as brewing.

Unfortunately, *BeeR, the magazine* lasted only 11 issues over two years. After multiple disputes, Bill Owens fired some of his editorial staff, who turned around and sued him, asserting that they were half-owners of *BeeR, the magazine* and *American Brewer*. A judgment found Owens Publishing to be worth $2,000,000, and that Owens owed the plaintiffs half of that. Owens continued to fight in court.[171] As Geoff Harries remembered, "[Owens] spread himself too thin and didn't want the headache of running Buffalo Bill's Brewery, which is when I purchased it" in 1994.[172] *BeeR, the magazine* stopped publication in 1995, and Owens focused on *American Brewer* and contract brewing. In 1997 Owens lost the lawsuit to Harries, and was forced to return contract brewing of Buffalo Bill's beer to Buffalo Bill's Brewery. About this time Owens purchased his antique shop and moved publishing of *American Brewer* to the back office.[173] By 2001, his antiques business was suffering due to eBay so he closed the store. Without a publishing home, Bill Owens, a pioneer in the craft beer world, was done with the industry. Owens sold *American Brewer* for $19,000 (a paltry sum compared to the judgment seven years earlier) to Bill Metzger, a beer writer who previously wrote articles for *American Brewer* along with other publications.[174] Metzger, as the publisher of the *Brewing News* network of regional consumer-focused newspapers based out of Buffalo, New York, added *American Brewer*, a trade magazine, to his roster of publications.[175] Bill Owens hopped in the car with the money and his camera and drove across the country, visiting brewer and industry friends for one last time, closing a twenty-year chapter of his life. Little did he know that same trip would lead to bigger and better things.

CONCLUSION

Though Owens is firmly and completely out of the photography and craft beer business, his experiences inform his current venture, American Distilling Institute (ADI), founded in 2003. During the trip across America funded by the sale of *American Brewer*, Owens visited and photographed some of the small, independent, and traditional distilleries that he was introduced to when creating the *American Brewer and Distiller Directory*. After returning from his trip, Owens was having a beer at the Bistro (a craft beer bar that opened in 1994 down the street from Buffalo Bill's that hosts numerous annual hoppy beer festivals) when he chatted with a young man reading a book on how to flip real estate.[176] Owens concluded that he was not chasing a dream, only chasing money. Owens declared that he would start a new business that he was passionate about. He went directly to the Alameda County Clerk-Recorder's Office and filed a fictitious business name or DBA for American Distilling Institute, LLC, (ADI) and started the process of setting up "the voice of craft distilling."[177]

ADI promotes craft spirit producers, independently-owned distilleries who produce fewer than 52,000 cases of liquor per year using tradition methods.[178] ADI offers legal advocacy and hosts conferences, workshops, and spirits competitions. Owens publishes *Distiller* magazine, an annual directory of craft distillers, and White Mule Press, a niche producer of publications about spirits. ADI's first event at St. George Spirits in Alameda, California had 77 participants interested in hearing about craft spirits. In 2017, 802 craft spirits from numerous US and international small, independent, and traditional distilleries were entered in numerous categories at the 11th Annual Judging of Craft Spirits. Through the American Distilling Institute, Owens continues to inspire creative, independent entrepreneurs in a craft industry.

In 2009 Owens published photographs from the initial road trip in *The Art of Distilling Whiskey and Other Spirits: An Enthusiast's Guide to the Artisan Distilling of Potent Potables*. Fritz Maytag of Anchor Brewing provided the foreword to the book since he, like Owens, shifted his focus to distilling when he opened the first craft distillery in 1993. Maytag said of Owens, "[h]e was one of the most fervent innovators. His own achievements are many, and his enthusiasms for the world wide explosion of brewing creativity is evidences in his obvious enjoyment of the successes of his brewing colleagues. [...] Bill and his cohorts are at it again, now celebrating a small-distillery revolution and the variety and creativity that is springing up everywhere."[179]

Bill Owens is a pioneer in craft beer whose influence continues to be felt sixteen years after his departure from the industry. He inspired generations of brewers, homebrewers, and beer fans through his publications, including *How to Build a Small Brewery: Draft Beer in Ten Days, American Brewer: The Business of Beer*, and *BeeR, the magazine*, where he gave a voice for many new writers and new ideas. He helped change laws on the state and national levels to ease the entry into the industry. He opened Buffalo Bill's Brewery, the third brewpub in the country and he created the modern concept of fresh beer served straight to the customer. There are now over 1,650 brewpubs in the US, many of which are part of the mother brewery/satellite or franchise system that Owens attempted and advocated. Owens re-introduced pumpkin ales to consumers as well as the every-increasing hoppiness of India Pale Ales and Imperial India Pale Ales. To the non-beer-drinker these may be the most obvious outcomes of Owens legacy, as supermarket shelves ebb and flow with a constant stream of new and/or seasonal products.

Brendan Moylan felt Owens' legacy was split between the how-to guide and the brewpub concept.[180] Brian Hunt said Bill's biggest innovation was Buffalo Bill's offering a different flavor than customers had ever tasted before.[181] Fall Allen said, "No other person that I can think of was involved on as many levels as Bill was."[182] Bill Metzger said, "Bill's creativity and foresight are exactly characteristic of what the industry embodies, that having made it the new face of beer—quality and creativity."[183]

While Owens is a pioneer whose legacy is felt in every aspect of the modern craft beer movement, he is not well known by younger drinkers because he is no longer in the beer industry. He continues to provide interviews about his photography and brewing days because he enjoys telling stories about his adventures. Like pioneers in many fields, he was among the first to explore craft beer but he continued to move on, never settling down.

Fig 29. Bill Owens, Bill in Full-Bill Mode. No Date, Black and White
Photograph. Bill Owens Personal Archives.

Bibliography

ARCHIVAL MATERIALS

Owens, Bill. "The Brewery." June 1983. Bill Owens Personal Archives.

———. "California Brew Pub, Limited (A California Limited Partnership) Certificate of Limited Partnership." January 12, 1983. Bill Owens Personal Archives.

———. "The Brew Pub Prospectus." July 24, 1982. Bill Owens Personal Archives.

BOOKS

Acitelli, Tom. *The Audacity of Hops: The History of America's Craft Beer Revolution.* Chicago, IL: Chicago Review Press, 2013.

Bamforth, Charles W.. "Maytag, Fritz." In *The Oxford Companion to Beer,* edited by Garrett Oliver, 581. New York, NY: Oxford University Press, 2012.

Baum, Dan. *Citizen Coors: A Grand Family Saga of Business, Politics, and Beer.* New York, NY: William Morrow, 2000.

Bjergsø, Mikkel Borg, and Pernille Pang. *Mikkeller's Book of Beer.* London, UK: Jacqui Small, 2015.

Brooks, Jay R. *California Breweries North.* Mechanicsburg, PA: Stackpole Books, 2013.

———. "Papazian, Charles." In *The Oxford Companion to Beer,* edited by Garrett Oliver, 640-641. New York, NY: Oxford University Press, 2012.

Brown, Pete. "Prohibition." In *The Oxford Companion to Beer,* edited by Garrett Oliver, 670-671. New York, NY: Oxford University Press, 2012.

Calagione, Sam. *Brewing Up a Business: Adventures in Entrepreneurship from the Founder of Dogfish Head Craft Brewery.* Hoboken, NJ: John Wiley & Sons, 2005.

———. *Off-centered Leadership: The Dogfish Head Guide to Motivation, Collaboration & Smart Growth.* Hoboken, NJ: John Wiley & Sons, 2016.

Cantwell, Dick. "Brewpub." In *The Oxford Companion to Beer,* edited by Garrett Oliver, 171-175. New York, NY: Oxford University Press, 2012.

———. "New Albion Brewing Company." In *The Oxford Companion to Beer,* edited by Garrett Oliver, 606-607. New York, NY: Oxford University Press, 2012.

Daniels, Ray. *Designing Great Beers: The Ultimate Guide to Brewing Classic Beer Styles.* Boulder, CO: Brewers Publications, 1998.

Dornbusch, Horst. "Lagering." In *The Oxford Companion to Beer,* edited by Garrett Oliver, 532-534. New York, NY: Oxford University Press, 2012.

Grant, Bert. *The Ale Master: How I Pioneered America's Craft Brewing Industry, Opened the First Brewpub, Bucked Trends, and Enjoyed Every Minute of It.* Seattle, WA: Sasquatch Books, 1998.

Grossman, Ken. *Beyond the Pale: The Story of Sierra Nevada Brewing Co.* Hoboken, NJ: John Wiley & Sons, 2013.

Hieronymus, Stan. *Brewing Local: American-Grown Beer.* Boulder, CO: Brewers Publications, 2016.

———. *For the Love of Hops: The Practical Guide to Aroma, Bitterness, and the Culture of Hops.* Boulder, CO: Brewers Publications, 2012.

Hindy, Steve, and Tom Potter. *Beer School: Bottling Success at the Brooklyn Brewery.* Hoboken, NJ: John Wiley & Sons, 2005.

Josephson, Marika, Aaron Kleidon, and Ryan Tockstein. *The Homebrewer's Almanac: A Seasonal Guide to Making Your Own Beer from Scratch.* New York, NY: The Countryman Press, 2016.

Knoedelseder, William. *Bitter Brew: The Rise and Fall of Anheuser-Busch and America's Kings of Beer.* New York, NY: HarperBusiness, 2012.

Koch, Greg, Steve Wagner, and Randy Clemens. *The Craft of Stone Brewing Co.: Liquid Lore, Epic Recipes, and Unabashed Arrogance.* Berkeley, CA: Ten Speed Press, 2011.

Koch, Jim. *Quench Your Own Thirst: Business Lessons Learned Over a Beer or Two.* New York, NY: Flatiron Books, 2016.

Krebs, Peter. *Redhook: Beer Pioneer.* New York, NY: Four Walls Eight Windows, 1998.

Magee, Tony. *So You Want to Start a Brewery?: The Lagunitas Story,* 2nd ed. Chicago, IL: Chicago Review Press, 2014.

Mallett, John. *Malt: A Practical Guide from Field to Brewhouse.* Boulder, CO: Brewers Publications, 2014.

Maytag, Fritz, foreword to *The Art of Distilling Whiskey and Other Spirits: An Enthusiast's Guide to the Artisan Distilling of Potent Potables,* eds. Bill Owens and Alan S. Dikty. Beverly, MA: Quarry Books, 2009.

Mosher, Randy. *Tasting Beer: An Insider's Guide to the World's Greatest Drink.* North Adams, MA: Storey Publishing, 2009.

Ogle, Maureen. *Ambitious Brew: The Story of American Beer.* Orlando, FL: Harvest Books, 2007.

Oliver, Garrett. *The Brewmaster's Table: Discovering the Pleasures of Real Beer with Real Food.* New York, NY: Ecco, 2005.

———. "Contract Brewing." In *The Oxford Companion to Beer,* edited by Garrett Oliver, 262-263. New York, NY: Oxford University Press, 2012.

———. "Craft Brewing." In *The Oxford Companion to Beer,* edited by Garrett Oliver, 270-273. New York, NY: Oxford University Press, 2012.

———. "Microbrewery." In *The Oxford Companion to Beer,* edited by Garrett Oliver, 585-586. New York, NY: Oxford University Press, 2012.

Owens, Bill. *How to Build a Small Brewery: Draft Beer in Ten Days,* 3rd ed. Hayward, CA: White Mule Press, 2009.

Owens, Bill, and Alan S. Dikty, eds. *The Art of Distilling Whiskey and Other Spirits: An Enthusiast's Guide to the Artisan Distilling of Potent Potables.* Beverly, MA: Quarry Books, 2009.

Palmer, John, and Colin Kaminski. *Water: A Comprehensive Guide for Brewers.* Boulder, CO: Brewers Publications, 2013.

Papazian, Charlie. *The Complete Joy of Homebrewing* Fourth Edition: Fully Revised and Updated. New York, NY: William Morrow, 2014.

Philliskirk, George. "Grundy Tank." In *The Oxford Companion to Beer,* edited by Garrett Oliver, 411. New York, NY: Oxford University Press, 2012.

Rabin, Dan, and Carl Forget, comps. *Dictionary of Beer and Brewing,* 2nd ed. Boulder, CO:

Brewers Publications, 1998.

Slosberg, Pete. *Beer for Pete's Sake: the Wicked Adventures of a Brewing Maverick*. Boulder, CO: Siris Books, 1998.

Van Munching, Philip. *Beer Blast: The Inside Story of the Brewing Industry's Bizarre Battles for Your Money*. New York, NY: Times Business, 1997.

Watt, James. *Business for Punks: Break All the Rules—the BrewDog Way*. New York, NY: Portfolio, 2016.

White, Chris, and Jamil Zainasheff. *Yeast: The Practical Guide to Beer Fermentation*. Boulder, CO: Brewers Publications, 2010.

INTERVIEWS AND PERSONAL COMMUNICATION

Allen, Fal. E-mail message to author. February 29, 2016.

Bates, Thomas. Interview by Patrick Walls, March 7, 2016.

Harries, Geoff. E-mail message to author. March 25, 2016.

Hunt, Brian. Interview by Patrick Walls, February 25, 2016.

Lewis, Michael. E-mail message to author, March 6, 2016.

———. E-mail message to author, March 10, 2016.

Metzger, Bill. E-mail message to author, August 24, 2016.

Moylan, Brendan. Interview by Patrick Walls, March 15, 2016.

Owens, Bill. Interview by Patrick Walls, January 9, 2016.

———. Interview by Patrick Walls, January 23, 2016.

Papazian, Charlie. E-mail message to author, March 4, 2016.

JOURNALS, MAGAZINES, NEWSPAPERS

Cantwell, Dick. "Book Review." *American Brewer: The Business of Beer*. No 65, 1995.

———. "Letters: Our Readers Respond." *American Brewer: The Business of Beer*. No. 58, Sprung, 1994.

Dodsworth, Fred. "FrEdit Speak." *American Brewer: The Business of Beer*. No 54, Winter, 1993.

Edwards, Owen. "Sure Shot: Bill Owens Was Seeking a Fresh Take on Suburban Life When He Spied Young Richie Ferguson." *Smithsonian*, October, 2010.

Hagen, Charles. "John Collier Jr., 78, A Teacher, Writer and Photographer." *New York Times*, March 5, 1992.

Least Heat Moon, William. "A Glass of Handmade." *Atlantic Monthly*. November, 1987.

McAuliffe, Jack, and Fred Eckhardt. "Letters." *Home Fermenter's Digest: The Home Brewing & Fermentation Magazine*. December, 1985.

Owens, Bill. "Bill Owens: Brewpub Consultant Advertisement." *American Brewer: The Micro-Brewer/Brew Pub Magazine*. Vol 3, No 35. Winter 1987.

———. "BillSpeak: The Most Fun You Can Have." *American Brewer: The Micro-Brewer/Brewpub Magazine*. Summer 1989.

———. "BillSpeak: Reg. 'D': One Million Dollars." *American Brewer: The Business of Beer*. Issue 45. Summer 1990.

———. "Editorial." *Amateur Brewer: The Micro-Brewer/Brew Pub Magazine*. Fall 1986.

———. "Editorial." *American Brewer* and *Distiller Directory*. 2000.

———. "Editorial." *Home Fermenter's Digest: The Home Brewing & Fermentation Magazine*. Vol 5, No 3. May/June, 1985.

———. "Editorial: Setting the Record Straight." *American Brewer: The Business of Beer.* Vol 16, No 3. September/October 2000.

———. "Letters." *American Brewer: The Micro-Brewer/Brewpub Magazine.* Summer 1988.

———. "Publican's Corner." *BEER: The Magazine.* Vol. 1, No 1, 1993.

———. "The Brewpub Manual Advertisement." *American Brewer: The Micro-Brewer/Brew Pub Magazine.* Vol 3, No 35. Winter 1987.

———. "Trademarking the Word 'Brewpub.'" *Amateur Brewer: The Micro-Brewer/Brew Pub Magazine.* Fall 1986.

Stewart, Hank. "The Tale of the Alpha King Challenge." *American Brewer: The Business of Beer.* Vol 15, No 4. December 2000.

WEBSITES

"2015 Small & Independent U.S. Craft Brewers' Growth in the Beer Category." *Brewers Association.* March 22, 2016. https://www.brewersassociation.org/press-releases/2015-craft-beer-data- infographic/.

"About the Draught Board." *Draught Board Homebrew Club.* Accessed March 1, 2016. http://www.draughtboard.org.

"Alpha King Challenge: Who Will Be Crowned in a Battle of the Brews?" *YCH Hops LLC,* accessed January 13, 2017. https://ychhops.com/connect/events/alpha-king-challenge.

"American Distilling Institute." *American Distilling Institute.* Accessed March 1, 2016. http://www.distilling.com.

"Anheuser-Busch InBev 2015 Annual Report." *Anheuser-Busch InBev.* Accessed April 16, 2016. http://www.abinbev.com/content/dam/universaltemplate/abinbev/pdf/investors/annual-and-hy-reports/2015/Commercial-Part-ENG.pdf

"Beer Styles." *Brewers Publications.* Accessed March 21, 2017. http://brewerspublications.com/category/beer-styles/.

"Bison Organic Beer: More than a Beer, a Movement." *Bison Brewery.* Accessed March 1, 2016. bisonbrew.com/themovement/.

"Brews and News November 1978." *Maltose Falcons.* Accessed March 1, 2016. https://www.maltosefalcons.com/sites/default/files/V3%238%2011-78.pdf.

"Buffalo Bill's Brewery 2015." *Buffalo Bill's Brewery.* 2015. http://buffalobillsbrewery.com/img/assets/2015-Buffalo-Bill's-Brochure.pdf/.

"Craft Brewer Definition." *Brewers Association.* Accessed April 16, 2016. https://www.brewersassociation.org/brewers-association/craft-brewer-definition/.

"Craft Beer Industry Market Segments." *Brewers Association.* July 1, 2016. https://www.brewersassociation.org/statistics/market-segments/.

Clark, Krissy. "Not So Bezerkeley After All." *American Public Media: Weekend America.* May 17, 2008. http://weekendamerica.publicradio.org/display/web/2008/05/15/bezerkeley.

"Draught Beer Quality Manual, 2nd ed." *Brewers Association.* 2011. Accessed March 21, 2016. http://www.draughtquality.org/wpcontent/uploads/2012/ 01/DQM_Full_Final.pdf.

"Great Pumpkin Beer Fest." *Elysian Brewing.* Accessed March 1, 2016. http://www.elysianbrewing.com/calendar/great-pumpkin-beer-fest/.

Lang, Doug. "Photographer, Brew Master, Publisher: Bill Owens Comes Full Circle." *Art a Gogo.* 2000. http://www.artagogo.com/interview/owensinterview/owensinterview.htm.

"Number of Breweries: Historical US Brewery Count." *Brewers Association.* 2016. https://www.brewersassociation.org/statistics/number-of-breweries/.

Owens, Bill. "Craft Certification." *American Distilling Institute*. Accessed March 21, 2016. http://distilling.com/resources/craft-certification/.

———. "The Short Bill Owens Biography." *Bill Owens: Photographer*. 2014. http://www.billowens.com/short-bio/.

"Small and Independent Brewers Continue to Grow Double Digits." *Brewers Association*. March 22, 2016. https://www.brewersassociation.org/press-releases/small-independent- brewers-continue-grow-double-digits/.

"The Year in Beer: U.S. Brewery Count Reaches All-Time High of 4,144." *Brewers Association*. December 2, 2015. https://www.brewersassociation.org/press-releases/the-year-in-beer-u-s- brewery-count-reaches-all-time-high-of-4144/.

Vandenengel, Heather. "Pumpkin Power: The Rise and Reign of Pumpkin Beer." *All About Beer Magazine*. Vol 35, Issue 5. October 1, 2014. http://allaboutbeer.com/article/pumpkin-beer/.

Watson, Bart. "The Brewpub Advantage." *Brewers Association*. February 17, 2016. https://www.brewersassociation.org/articles/the-brewpub-advantage/.

———. "Economic Impact." *Brewers Association*. Accessed January 24, 2017. https://www.brewersassociation.org/statistics/economic-impact-data/.

———. "November: Pumpkin Beers Die & Specialty Releases Thrive." *Brewers Association*. November 2, 2015. https://www.brewersassociation.org/insights/november-beers/.

ENDNOTES

1   Garrett Oliver, *The Brewmaster's Table: Discovering the Pleasures of Real Beer with Real Food*, (New York, NY: Ecco, 2005), 43.

2   "Craft Brewer Definition," *Brewers Association*, accessed April 16, 2016. https://www.brewersassociation.org/brewers-association/craft-brewer-definition/.

3   "Anheuser-Busch InBev 2015 Annual Report," *Anheuser-Busch InBev*, accessed April 16, 2016. http://www.ab-inbev.com/content/dam/universaltemplate/abinbev/pdf/investors/annual-and-hy-reports/2015/Commercial-Part-ENG.pdf.

4   "Small and Independent Brewers Continue to Grow Double Digits," *Brewers Association*, March 22, 2016. https://www.brewersassociation.org/press-releases/small-independent-brewers-continue-grow-double-digits/.

5   "Craft Beer Industry Market Segments," *Brewers Association*, July 1, 2016. https://www.brewersassociation.org/statistics/market-segments/.

6   Ibid.

7   "The Year in Beer: U.S. Brewery Count Reaches All-Time High of 4,144," *Brewers Association*, December 2, 2015. https://www.brewersassociation.org/press-releases/the-year-in-beer-u-s-brewery-count-reaches-all-time-high-of-4144/.

8   See Maureen Ogle's *Ambitious Brew: The Story of American Beer*, 2007 for a concise history.

9   "The Year in Beer."

10   "2015 Small & Independent U.S. Craft Brewers' Growth in the Beer Category," *Brewers Association*, March 22, 2016. https://www.brewersassociation.org/press-releases/2015-craft-beer-data-infographic/.

11   Bart Watson, "Economic Impact," *Brewers Association*, accessed January 24, 2017, https://www.brewersassociation.org/statistics/economic-impact-data/.

12   Maureen Ogle, *Ambitious Brew: The Story of American Beer*. (Orlando, FL: Harvest Books, 2007); Tom Acitelli, *The Audacity of Hops: The History of America's Craft Beer Revolution*. (Chicago, IL: Chicago Review Press, 2013); Dan Baum, *Citizen Coors: A Grand Family Saga of Business, Politics, and Beer*. (New York, NY: William Morrow, 2000); William Knoedelseder, *Bitter Brew: The Rise and Fall of Anheuser-Busch and America's Kings of Beer*. (New York, NY: HarperBusiness, 2012); Philip Van Munching, *Beer Blast: The Inside Story of the Brewing Industry's Bizarre Battles for Your Money*. (New York, NY: Times Business, 1997); Ken Grossman, *Beyond the Pale: The Story of Sierra Nevada Brewing Co.* (Hoboken, NJ: John Wiley & Sons, 2013); Steve Hindy and Tom Potter, *Beer School: Bottling Success at the Brooklyn Brewery*. (Hoboken, NJ: John Wiley & Sons, 2005); Sam Calagione, *Brewing Up a Business: Adventures in Entrepreneurship from the Founder of Dogfish Head Craft Brewery*. (Hoboken, NJ: John Wiley & Sons, 2005); Sam Calagione, *Off-centered Leadership: The Dogfish Head Guide to Motivation, Collaboration & Smart Growth*. (Hoboken, NJ: John Wiley & Sons, 2016); Tony Magee,

So You Want to Start a Brewery?: The Lagunitas Story, 2nd ed. (Chicago, IL: Chicago Review Press, 2014); Jim Koch, *Quench Your Own Thirst: Business Lessons Learned Over a Beer or Two.* (New York, NY: Flatiron Books, 2016); Bert Grant, *The Ale Master: How I Pioneered America's Craft Brewing Industry, Opened the First Brewpub, Bucked Trends, and Enjoyed Every Minute of It.* (Seattle, WA: Sasquatch Books, 1998); Peter Krebs, Redhook: Beer Pioneer. (New York, NY: Four Walls Eight Windows, 1998); Pete Slosberg, *Beer for Pete's Sake: The Wicked Adventures of a Brewing Maverick.* (Boulder, CO: Siris Books, 1998); Greg Koch, Steve Wagner, and Randy Clemens, *The Craft of Stone Brewing Co.: Liquid Lore, Epic Recipes, and Unabashed Arrogance.* (Berkeley, CA: Ten Speed Press, 2011); Mikkel Borg Bjergsø and Pernille Pang, *Mikkeller's Book of Beer.* (London, UK: Jacqui Small, 2015); James Watt, *Business for Punks: Break All the Rules—the BrewDog Way.* (New York, NY: Portfolio, 2016); Marika Josephson, Aaron Kleidon, and Ryan Tockstein, *The Homebrewer's Almanac: A Seasonal Guide to Making Your Own Beer from Scratch.* (New York, NY: The Countryman Press, 2016).

13   For a current list of 35 recipe/history books on beer styles published by the Brewers Association see "Beer Styles," *Brewers Publications,* accessed March 21, 2017, http://www. brewerspublications.com/category/beer-styles/.

14   John Mallett, *Malt: A Practical Guide from Field to Brewhouse,* (Boulder, CO: Brewers Publications, 2014), 9-11.

15   Stan Hieronymus, *For the Love of Hops: The Practical Guide to Aroma, Bitterness and the Culture of Hops,* (Boulder, CO: Brewers Publications, 2012), 38.

16   Chris White and Jamil Zainasheff, *Yeast: The Practical Guide to Beer Fermentation,* (Boulder, CO: Brewers Publications, 2010), 34.

17   John Palmer and Colin Kaminski, *Water: A Comprehensive Guide for Brewers,* (Boulder, CO: Brewers Publications, 2013), 156-159.

18   Garrett Oliver, "Craft Brewing," in *The Oxford Companion to Beer,* ed. Garrett Oliver (New York, NY: Oxford University Press, 2012), 272.

19   Ogle, *Ambitious Brew,* 259-261.

20   Charles W. Bamforth, "Maytag, Fritz," in *The Oxford Companion to Beer,* ed. Garrett Oliver (New York, NY: Oxford University Press, 2012), 581.

21   Acitelli, *The Audacity of Hops,* 11.

22   Ibid, 25.

23   McAuliffe took umbrage with the assertion made by Fred Eckhardt, a noted beer writer, that McAuliffe was influenced by Maytag. He responded to an article by Eckhardt with a letter to the editor stating, "[t]his statement by Mr. Eckhardt, which you published, is false and libelous. I was not inspired by Mr. Maytag's success to start the New Albion Brewing Company." Eckhardt responded by saying "I was proud of McAuliffe's accomplishment [...] McAuliffe's success is measured by the success of others: Red Hook and Sierra Nevada for examples, rather than by his own, because without his sacrifice, the others might not have begun at all." He later says "I am also sorry I accused you of taking inspiration from Fritz Maytag. He has been an inspiration to nearly everyone else in the small beer business—I do apologize for that assumption." See Jack McAuliffe and Fred Eckhardt, "Letters," *Home Fermenter's Digest: The Home Brewing & Fermentation Magazine,* December 1985, 4-5.

24   Dick Cantwell, "New Albion Brewing Company," in *The Oxford Companion to Beer,* ed. Garrett Oliver (New York, NY: Oxford University Press, 2012), 606-607.

25   Acitelli, *The Audacity of Hops,* 45.

26   Ibid., 70.

27   Cantwell, "New Albion Brewing Company," 606.

28   Eckhardt, "Letters," 4-5.

29   Randy Mosher, *Tasting Beer: An Insider's Guide to the World's Greatest Drink,* (North Adams,

MA: Storey Publishing, 2009), 212.

30   Michael Lewis, e-mail message to author, March 10, 2016.

31   Hieronymus, *For the Love of Hops*, 189.

32   Lewis, March 10.

33   Michael Lewis, e-mail message to author, March 6.

34   Dick Cantwell, "Book Review," *American Brewer: The Business of Beer*, no. 65 (1995): 52.

35   Acitelli, *The Audacity of Hops*, 18.

36   Ibid., 58.

37   Ogle, *Ambitious Brew*, 279.

38   Jay R. Brooks, "Papazian, Charles," in *The Oxford Companion to Beer*, ed. Garrett Oliver (New York, NY: Oxford University Press, 2012), 640-641.

39   Krissy Clark, "Not So Bezerkeley After All," *American Public Media: Weekend America*, May 17, 2008. http://weekendamerica.publicradio.org/display/web/2008/05/15/bezerkeley.

40   Thomas Bates, interview by Patrick Walls, March 7, 2016.

41   "Brews and News November 1978," *Maltose Falcons*, accessed March 1, 2016, https://www.maltosefalcons.com/sites/default/files/V3%238%2011-78.pdf.

42   Garrett Oliver, "Microbrewery," in *The Oxford Companion to Beer*, ed. Garrett Oliver (New York, NY: Oxford University Press, 2012), 586.

43   Dan Rabin and Carl Forget, comps., *Dictionary of Beer & Brewing*, 2nd ed. (Boulder, CO: Brewers Publications, 1998), 264.

44   Ogle, *Ambitious Brew*, 205.

45   Pete Brown, "Prohibition," in *The Oxford Companion to Beer*, ed. Garrett Oliver (New York, NY: Oxford University Press, 2012), 671.

46   Acitelli, *The Audacity of Hops*, 70.

47   George Philliskirk, "Grundy Tank," in *The Oxford Companion to Beer*, ed. Garrett Oliver (New York, NY: Oxford University Press, 2012), 411.

48   Charlie Papazian, *The Complete Joy of Homebrewing Fourth Edition: Fully Revised and Updated*, (New York, NY: William Morrow, 2014), 15.

49   Bill Owens, interview with Pat Walls, January 9, 2016.

50   Charles Hagen, "John Collier Jr., 78, A Teacher, Writer and Photographer," *New York Times* (New York, NY), March 5, 1992.

51   Ibid.

52   Owen Edwards, "Sure Shot: Bill Owens Was Seeking a Fresh Take on Suburban Life When He Spied Young Richie Ferguson," *Smithsonian*, October, 2010, 11.

53   Bill Owens, "The Short Bill Owens Biography," *Bill Owens: Photographer*, 2014. http://www.billowens.com/short-bio/.

54   Bill Owens, interview with Pat Walls, January 9, 2016.

55   Ibid.

56   Bill Owens, *How to Build a Small Brewery: Draft Beer in Ten Days*, 3rd ed. (Hayward, CA: White Mule Press, 2009), v.

57   Mallett, *Malt*, 114.

58   Rabin and Forget, *Dictionary of Beer & Brewing*, 180-181.

59   Bill Owens, interview with Pat Walls, January 9, 2016.

60   Papazian, *The Complete Joy of Homebrewing*, 141.

61   See Hieronymus, *For the Love of Hops*, for a book-length discussion.

62   Owens, *How to Build a Small Brewery*, 14.

63   White and Zainasheff, *Yeast*, 41-42.

64   Hieronymus, *For the Love of Hops*, 74.

65   Horst Dornbusch, "Lagering," in *The Oxford Companion to Beer*, ed. Garrett Oliver (New York, NY: Oxford University Press, 2012), 533-534.

66   Owens, *How to Build a Small Brewery*, 26-27.

67   Charlie Papazian, e-mail message to author, March 4, 2016.

68   Brendan Moylan, interview with Pat Walls, March 15, 2016.

69   Acitelli, *The Audacity of Hops*, 172, 231.

70   "Buffalo Bill's Brewery 2015," *Buffalo Bill's Brewery*, 2015, http://buffalobillsbrewery.com/img/assets/2015-Buffalo-Bill's-Brochure.pdf.

71   Bill Owens, interview with Pat Walls, January 23, 2016.

72   Acitelli, *The Audacity of Hops*, 85.

73   Dick Cantwell, "Brewpub," in *The Oxford Companion to Beer*, ed. Garrett Oliver (New York, NY: Oxford University Press, 2012), 173.

74   Bill Owens, interview with Pat Walls, January 23, 2016.

75   Charlie Papazian, e-mail message to author, March 4, 2016.

76   Cantwell, "Brewpub," 172.

77   Tom Bates, interview with Pat Walls, March 7, 2016.

78   Ibid.

79   Bill Owens, interview with Pat Walls, January 9, 2016.

80   Bill Owens, "The Brew Pub Prospectus," July 24, 1982. Bill Owens Personal Archives.

81   Bill Owens, interview with Pat Walls, January 9, 2016.

82   Bill Owens, "California Brew Pub, Limited (A California Limited Partnership) Certificate of Limited Partnership," January 12, 1983. Bill Owens Personal Archives.

83   Bill Owens, "The Brewery," June, 1983. Bill Owens Personal Archives.

84   Acitelli, *The Audacity of Hops*, 98-101.

85   Bill Owens, interview with Pat Walls, January 9, 2016.

86   Ibid.

87   Ibid.

88   Ibid.

89   Mallett, *Malt*, 119-120.

90   Brendan Moylan, interview with Pat Walls, March 15, 2016.

91   Hieronymus, *For the Love of Hops*, 277.

92   Bill Owens, interview with Pat Walls, January 9, 2016.

93   Mosher, *Tasting Beer*, 133.

94   Brian Hunt, interview with Pat Walls, February 25, 2016.

95   Ibid.

96   Brendan Moylan, interview with Pat Walls, March 15, 2016.

97   A glycol system keeps beer chilled between serving tanks or kegs and the taps. Beer lines are insulated along with tubes of chilled glycol, a food-grade refrigerant, to maintain the beer temperature between the serving tanks and the taps. This is necessary for tap lines longer than 25 feet as longer distances affect the gas pressure and temperature which causes foaming issues. See "Draught Beer

Quality Manual, 2nd ed.," *Brewers Association*, 2011, accessed March 21, 2017, 32-33. http://www.draughtquality.org/wp-content/uploads/2012/01/DQM_Full_Final.pdf.

98   Bill Owens, interview with Pat Walls, January 9, 2016.

99   Ibid.

100   Bill Owens, interview with Pat Walls, January 9, 2016.

101   Ibid.

102   Bill Owens, interview with Pat Walls, January 9, 2016.

103   William Least Heat Moon, "A Glass of Handmade," *Atlantic Monthly*, November, 1987, 85.

104   Ibid, 86.

105   Bill Owens, interview with Pat Walls, January 9, 2016.

106   Buffalo Bill's Brewery Press Release in *American Brewer Magazine* as seen in "Buffalo Bill's Brewery 2015."

107   Bill Owens, interview with Pat Walls, January 9, 2016.

108   Heather Vandenengel, "Pumpkin Power: The Rise and Reign of Pumpkin Beer," *All About Beer Magazine*, Vol 35, Issue 5, October 1, 2014, 1. http://allaboutbeer.com/article/pumpkin-beer/.

109   Stan Hieronymus, *Brewing Local: American-Grown Beer*, (Boulder, CO: Brewers Publications, 2016), 227.

110   "Great Pumpkin Beer Fest," *Elysian Brewing*, accessed March 1, 2016. http://www.elysianbrewing.com/calendar/great-pumpkin-beer-fest/.

111   Vandenengel, "Pumpkin Power," 2.

112   Bart Watson, "November: Pumpkin Beers Die & Specialty Releases Thrive" *Brewers Association*, November 2, 2015. https://www.brewersassociation.org/insights/november-beers/.

113   Bill Owens, interview with Pat Walls, January 9, 2016.

114   Ibid.

115   Vandenengel, "Pumpkin Power," 2.

116   "Buffalo Bill's Brewery 2015."

117   Mosher, *Tasting Beer*, 212-213.

118   Bill Owens, interview with Pat Walls, January 9, 2016.

119   Ibid.

120   "Buffalo Bill's Brewery 2015."

121   Garrett Oliver, "Contract Brewing," in *The Oxford Companion to Beer*, ed. Garrett Oliver (New York, NY: Oxford University Press, 2012), 262.

122   Geoff Harries, e-mail message to author, March 25, 2016.

123   Bill Owens, interview with Pat Walls, January 23, 2016.

124   Bill Owens, "Trademarking the Word 'Brewpub,'" *Amateur Brewer: The Micro-Brewer/Brew Pub Magazine*, Fall, 1986, 40.

125   Brendan Moylan, interview with Pat Walls, March 15, 2016.

126   Bill Owens, interview with Pat Walls, January 23, 2016.

127   Ibid.

128   Geoff Harries, e-mail message to author, March 25, 2016.

129   Bill Owens, interview with Pat Walls, January 23, 2016.

130   Ibid.

131   Bill Owens, "BillSpeak: The Most Fun You Can Have," *American Brewer: The Micro-Brewer/Brewpub Magazine*, Summer, 1989, 52.

132   Ibid.

133   Ibid.

134   "Bison Organic Beer: More than a Beer, a Movement," *Bison Brewery*. Accessed March 1, 2016. bisonbrew.com/themovement/.

135   Bill Owens, interview with Pat Walls, January 9, 2016.

136   Bill Owens, "BillSpeak: Reg. 'D': One Million Dollars," *American Brewer: The Business of Beer*, Issue 45, Summer, 1990. 60.

137   Geoff Harries, e-mail message to author, March 25, 2016.

138   "Number of Breweries: Historical US Brewery Count," *Brewers Association*, 2016. https://www.brewersassociation.org/statistics/number-of-breweries/.

139   Bill Owens, interview with Pat Walls, January 23, 2016.

140   Geoff Harries, e-mail message to author, March 25, 2016.

141   Bill Owens, interview with Pat Walls, January 23, 2016.

142   Ibid.

143   Geoff Harries, e-mail message to author, March 25, 2016.

144   Bill Owens, interview with Pat Walls, January 23, 2016.

145   Ibid.

146   Bill Owens, "Editorial," *Home Fermenter's Digest: The Home Brewing and Fermentation Magazine*, Vol 5 No 3, May/June 1985, 2.

147   Owens, "Trademarking the Word 'Brewpub,'" *Amateur Brewer*, 40.

148   Bill Owens, "Editorial," *Amateur Brewer: The Micro-Brewer/Brew Pub Magazine*, Fall, 1986, 5.

149   Bill Owens, "Editorial: Setting the Record Straight," *American Brewer: The Business of Beer*, Vol 16, No 3, September/October, 2000, 6.

150   Bill Owens, "Letters," *American Brewer: The Micro-Brewer/Brewpub Magazine*, No 37, Summer, 1988, 6.

151   Bill Owens, interview with Pat Walls, January 23, 2016.

152   Ibid.

153   Charlie Papazian, e-mail message to author, March 4, 2016.

154   Ibid.

155   Fal Allen, e-mail message to author, February 29, 2016.

156   Dick Cantwell, "Letters: Our Readers Respond," *American Brewer: The Business of Beer*, No 58, Sprung, 1994, 10.

157   Brendan Moylan, interview with Pat Walls, March 15, 2016.

158   Acitelli, *The Audacity of Hops*, 190.

159   Bill Owens, interview with Pat Walls, January 23, 2016.

160   Bill Owens, "Publican's Corner," *BEER: The Magazine*, Vol 1, No 1, 1993, 4.

161   Fred Dodsworth, "FrEdit Speak," *American Brewer: The Business of Beer*, No 54, Winter, 1993, 4.

162   Owens, "Publican's Corner," 1993, 4.

163   Bill Owens, interview with Pat Walls, January 23, 2016.

164   Ibid.

165   Hank Stewart, "The Tale of the Alpha King Challenge," *American Brewer: The Business of Beer*, Vol 15, No 4, December, 2000, 7-8.

166 "Alpha King Challenge: Who Will Be Crowned in a Battle of the Brews?" *YCH Hops LLC*, accessed January 13, 2017. https://ychhops.com/connect/events/alpha-king-challenge.

167 Bill Owens, "The Brewpub Manual Advertisement," *American Brewer: The Micro-Brewer/ Brew Pub Magazine*, Vol 3, No 35, Winter, 1987, 13.

168 Bill Owens, "Bill Owens: Brewpub Consultant Advertisement," *American Brewer: The Micro-Brewer/Brew Pub Magazine*, Vol 3, No 35, Winter, 1987, 46.

169 Bill Owens, interview with Pat Walls, January 9, 2016.

170 Bill Owens, "Editorial," *American Brewer* and *Distiller Directory*, 2000, 6.

171 Ibid.

172 Geoff Harries, e-mail message to author, March 25, 2016.

173 Bill Owens, interview with Pat Walls, January 23, 2016.

174 Ibid.

175 Bill Metzger, e-mail message to author, August 24, 2016.

176 Bill Owens, interview with Pat Walls, January 23, 2016.

177 "American Distilling Institute," *American Distilling Institute*, distilling.com.

178 Bill Owens, "Craft Certification," *American Distilling Institute*, accessed March 21, 2016. http://distilling.com/resources/craft-certification/.

179 Fritz Maytag, foreword to *The Art of Distilling Whiskey and Other Spirits: An Enthusiast's Guide to the Artisan Distilling of Potent Potables*, eds. Bill Owens and Alan S. Dikty (Beverly, MA: Quarry Books, 2009), 9.

180 Brendan Moylan, interview with Pat Walls, March 15, 2016.

181 Brian Hunt, interview with Pat Walls, February 25, 2016.

182 Fal Allen, e-mail message to author, February 29, 2016.

183 Bill Metzger, e-mail message to author, August 24, 2016.

www.ingramcontent.com/pod-product-compliance
Lightning Source LLC
Chambersburg PA
CBHW042338040426

42447CB00018B/3477